WASHINGTON'S NIGHTMARE:

A Brief History of American Political Parties

B. SCOTT CHRISTMAS

Published by CreateSpace: An Amazon Company
Seattle, Washington
Charleston, South Carolina
www.createspace.com

Washington's Nightmare: A Brief History of American Political Parties. Copyright © 2014 by Scott Christmas. All rights reserved. This book or any portion thereof may not be reproduced or used in any manner whatsoever without the express written permission of the publisher except for the use of brief quotations in a book review.

First Print Edition August 2017

ISBN: 978-1522004738

TABLE OF CONTENTS

Introduction	6

Political Parties of the 19th Century:

THE FEDERALIST PARTY	10
THE DEMOCRATIC-REPUBLICAN PARTY	16
THE 19TH CENTURY DEMOCRATIC PARTY	22
THE NATIONAL REPUBLICAN PARTY	28
THE ANTI-MASONIC PARTY	32
THE WHIG PARTY	36
THE LIBERTY PARTY AND THE FREE SOIL PARTY	44
THE 19TH CENTURY REPUBLICAN PARTY	52
THE AMERICAN PARTY	61
THE OPPOSITION PARTY AND THE CONSTITUTIONAL UNION PARTY	67
THE PEOPLE'S PARTY	71

Political Parties of the 20th and 21st Centuries:

THE SOCIALIST PARTY OF AMERICA	78
THE PROGRESSIVE PARTY	84

THE 20TH AND 21ST CENTURY
    REPUBLICAN PARTY   89
THE 20TH AND 21ST CENTURY
    DEMOCRATIC PARTY   98
THE STATES' RIGHTS DEMOCRATIC PARTY AND
    THE AMERICAN INDEPENDENT PARTY   106
THE LIBERTARIAN PARTY   112
THE REFORM PARTY   116
THE CONSTITUTION PARTY   120
THE GREEN PARTY   124

Afterword   127
Bibliography   132

May we not, then, hope that the long agitation [over slavery] is approaching its end, and that the geographical parties to which it has given birth, so much dreaded by the Father of His Country, will speedily become extinct?

~ James Buchanan, 1856

INTRODUCTION

POLITICAL PARTIES are a bit like religious denominations – they rarely form out of thin air, but instead tend to evolve over time.

This fact is easy to forget in this day and age when the United States is virtually wholly controlled by two prevailing parties, representing two prevailing political ideologies. For many of us, it may seem that these two parties have always existed and have always been just like they are today.

Nothing, of course, could be farther from the truth.

In the earliest days of the United States, there was no such thing as an organized political party that used resources and people power to help elect like-minded individuals. As such, the first few sessions of Congress in the 1790s, as well as the first presidency under George Washington, were all effectively non-partisan. It is difficult to imagine such a scenario today.

Political parties as we know them today were first formed on a wide basis in 17th century England. During that era, English politicians became increasingly divided over the role of Parliament in relation to the monarchy, and factions formed pitting so-called "Parliamentarians" against so-called "Royalists." These two factions eventually evolved (or devolved, as the case may be) into the first true political parties: the Whigs, who supported a stronger, democratic Parliament and thus a weaker monarch, and the Tories, who supported the autocratic and traditional rule of the king and aristocracy.

By the time the United States was formed in the late 18th century, the Founding Fathers had learned many lessons from their parent nation about the dangers of political parties and factions. Determined not to make the same mistakes, many early American statesmen urged their countrymen not to give in to the temptation of forming political parties. In his so-called "Farewell Address," at the end of his presidency in 1796, George Washington stated:

> This [tendency among people to form political coalitions]…is inseparable from our nature … But it is truly our worst enemy. The alternate domination of one faction over another…is itself a frightful despotism … The common and continual mischiefs of [political parties] are sufficient to make it in the interest and duty of a wise people to discourage and restrain [them].

Unfortunately, no one took the Father of His Nation very seriously on this point.

While it is true that organized political parties did not exist during the earliest days of the United States, factions had been forming since the end of the Revolutionary War on an issue that was eerily similar to the one confronted in England a century earlier: the role of state governments in relation to the national government – that is, federal government vs. local government.

The Articles of Confederation, drawn up in 1777 and ratified by 1781, had established the colonies as sovereign states in a perpetual union. Following the Revolutionary War and the achievement of true independence, however, many statesmen began arguing that the Articles were not sufficient to effectively run the nation (and, especially, to pay off war debt) because the federal government had virtually no power. This led to an ideological split and the formation of political factions. On the one hand were the so-called Federalists, who were in favor of a new constitution and a stronger national government. On the other were the Anti-Federalists, who favored maintaining the Articles of Confederation and thereby maintaining more sovereignty for the states.

Eventually, the Federalist perspective won the day, and a new constitution was drafted and ratified, going into effect on March 4, 1789. For several years thereafter, there was relative peace and accord among the leaders of the new country.

But those political factions of the 1780s, quarreling about the role of the federal government, had planted ideological seeds, and before Washington's first term was complete, the first real political parties had begun to sprout.

POLITICAL PARTIES OF THE 18TH AND 19TH CENTURIES

THE FEDERALIST PARTY

ALEXANDER HAMILTON, Secretary of the Treasury under George Washington, formed what would become the nation's first political party. He began his efforts as early as 1790; within a few years, his coalition was in full force and being referred to as the "Federalists." The name made sense: Hamilton's coalition was supported by many (but not all) of the same leaders and statesmen who had made up the Federalist movement of the previous decade, and who believed in a stronger federal government with more broad-based powers.

Hamilton's intention may never have been to create a true political party; instead, the party grew out of his efforts to enact a comprehensive economic program for the new country. Among other things, this program included the following:

1. The federal government would assume the debts of the states, both domestic debts and foreign debts. This amounted to roughly 54 million dollars, largely from loans and other expenses incurred during the Revolutionary War. Adjusted for inflation, this would amount to several trillion dollars today.
2. A national bank would be established to control these and other debts, and to regulate the economy.
3. The government would enact tariffs (taxes on products imported from other countries) and excise taxes (taxes on certain domestic products) in order to fund itself and pay off its debts.
4. The federal government would use its powers and resources to encourage manufacturing and, ultimately, the urbanization of its cities. This would include government subsidies to support the establishment and growth of manufacturing.

Through his position as Secretary of the Treasury, Hamilton was able to round up support across the country for this program, particularly among bankers and manufacturers, as well as among politicians who saw a much larger role for the federal government. As historian and political scientist William Chambers has noted, Hamilton's party began as a "capital" faction (existing in and around the nation's capital), then expanded through Hamilton's efforts to become a "national" faction, and finally, by the end of Washington's presidency, coalesced into a true political party.

Though this sort of political and economic program seems "normal" today, it was revolutionary and radical at the time, and there were many leaders within the government who opposed it. Their opposition was primarily an ideological one: it wasn't a question of whether it would *work* or not, it was a question of whether it was proper for the federal government to have this sort of power and influence in the economy of the states. In short, it became an issue not unlike the one faced by those who had drafted the Constitution a decade earlier – states' rights and privileges in relation to the power and privileges of the federal government.

By the time John Adams followed George Washington to the presidency, party politics were firmly in place. Adams was the first and, ultimately, only Federalist president in U.S. history. During his time in office the Federalists became heavily associated with the Hamilton economic program that had given birth to their movement, and in a more general sense became supporters of a more powerful central government, urbanization, and friendly relations with Great Britain. Their critics considered them self-righteous and autocratic, and criticized their disinterest in westward expansion of the new country. Federalists tended to support industry instead of agricultural interests, and were criticized for being a party of the aristocracy.

Perhaps the biggest criticism, in those early years, dealt with the perceived "monarchical" tendency of the Federalist leaders, particularly John Adams. Recall that the American people had just fought a war, less than two decades earlier, to defeat a monarchy that was seen as tyrannical. The last thing anyone wanted was to create a new government that devolved into a similar state of affairs.

And yet, to the critics of the Federalist Party, this was precisely what was happening.

In 1794, the Federalists approved the Jay Treaty with Great Britain, averting a possible return to hostilities, and establishing a trade alliance with America's former parent nation. This treaty outraged France, who, by that time, was involved in an effort to overthrow its own monarchy and establish a republican form of government similar to the one in the United States. Many Americans were sympathetic with the French cause and saw the Jay Treaty as pandering to "the enemy" at the expense of an important ally in France. Recall that France had been among the colonies' biggest supporters in the Revolutionary War with Great Britain.

The Jay Treaty, then, was seen by critics of the Federalists as a move in the wrong direction: a step toward monarchism and away from republicanism. Within four years, it ultimately strained relations with France so much that the U.S. ended up in a minor war with that country, which took place primarily at sea, and was sparked by French ships attacking U.S. merchant vessels trading with Great Britain.

Around this same time, things were getting even worse at home. Many state leaders opposed to the actions of Adams and the Federalists, and, viewing them as increasingly more tyrannical, began refusing to enforce national laws. Newspapers opposed to the Adams administration printed editorials criticizing the administration and encouraging uprisings and rebellions. The Federalists responded with one of the most controversial laws in U.S. history: the so-called Alien and Sedition Acts.

Convinced that much of the anti-Federalist sentiment among Americans was coming from, and encouraged by, French immigrants and their sympathizers (such as the Irish), the Alien and Sedition Acts were aimed largely at immigration. In addition to almost tripling the amount of time before a newly arrived immigrant could become a naturalized citizen, the laws also gave the president the right to deport any immigrant who came from a country the U.S. was at war with (in this case, France), and also permitted the president to deport *any* immigrant found to be "dangerous to the peace and safety of the United States."

Adams' controversial law also included an act aimed at his critics in the press, making it illegal to "write, print, utter, or publish...any false, scandalous, or malicious writing...against the United States" or any of its leaders. It also made it a crime to "excite...the hatred of the good people of the United States [against their leaders], or to stir up sedition within the United States." The penalty for conviction of such a crime was a fine up to two thousand dollars (an astronomical amount in 1798) and up to two years in prison.

Noticeably absent from this libel law was the person of the vice-president. The act explicitly made it a crime to criticize the president or Congress; there was no mention of the vice-president. This was no accident: the vice-president was Thomas Jefferson, one of the leaders of the movement against Adams and the Federalists. The presidency of 1797 to 1801 is the only one in history where the president and vice-president represented two different political parties (the Constitutional precedent that allowed this to happen was repealed by the 12th Amendment in 1803).

With one exception, all the laws made up by the Alien and Sedition Acts were either allowed to expire on their own (several had two-year expiration dates) or were repealed. That one exception, however, is the law giving the president the right to deport immigrants from nations at war with the United States. That law still exists in Title 50 of the United States Code.

Needless to say, the Alien and Sedition Acts did nothing to calm the partisan rhetoric surrounding Adams and the Federalists, and almost certainly led to the party losing its hold on power and forfeiting its broad-based support.

In 1800, Adams was challenged in his re-election bid by his own vice-president, Thomas Jefferson, and Jefferson defeated him. Never again would a Federalist own the presidency. Federalist legislators continued to serve in Congress for the next decade or two, but under Jefferson and his successors, their party began to wane. Following an interparty split over the War of 1812, the party collapsed. The last Federalist presidential candidate, Rufus King, ran in 1816, winning only three states and just 31% of the popular vote. According to electoral historian Kenneth C. Martis, the Federalists, in 1798, had held a 57% majority in the House of Representatives and nearly 70% in the Senate. That was the last Congressional term where Federalists held a majority in either chamber. In 1820, Federalists represented only 17% of the House, and just 8% of the Senate, and didn't even run a candidate in the presidential election that year (making James Monroe the only president other than George Washington to win a presidential election uncontested). By 1825, the Federalist Party had ceased to exist.

By the Numbers:

The Federalist Party

Founded: circa 1790-92

Period of Activity: Approximately 35 years at the federal level

Party Slogans: "Adams and Liberty;" "Peace and Commerce"

Number of Presidents: 1 (John Adams; George Washington was associated with, and sympathetic to, the Federalist Party platforms, but did not consider himself a member of any faction)

Leading Party Figures: Alexander Hamilton, John Adams, John Marshall (Chief Justice of the Supreme Court), Jonathan Dayton (4th Speaker of the House), Rufus King (U.S. Senator and perennial presidential and vice-presidential candidate)

Main Platforms: Banking, manufacturing, urbanization, strong federal government, support of industry over agriculture

THE DEMOCRATIC-REPUBLICAN PARTY

THE TERM "Democratic-Republican" is a modern one referring to the opposition party that arose against the Federalists in the 1790s. It is referred to in this way because contemporaries of the time frequently referred to it as the "Republican Party" and its members as "Republicans." Since this party is not affiliated with the Republican Party of the modern era, historians prefer to use a term with less potential for confusion.

In 1798, Thomas Jefferson wrote, in regards to the party's name: "[Members of the party] are styled Republicans, Whigs, [or] Jacobins." In letters and other writings, James Madison frequently referred to the group as the "Republican Party."

For these early opponents of the Federalist movement, "republican" referred not to a member of a widely-established political party with a widely-known platform, but instead referred to someone who supported a republican-style of government – that is, a representative government of the people – as opposed to a system (such as a monarchy or oligarchy) with power centralized for just a few.

In this way, of course, *all* the leading statesmen of the 1790s were republicans – no one was advocating a monarchy, and the United States government was undeniably a republic. So when the party opposed to the Federalists began calling themselves "republicans," it was a way of affirming their commitment to representative government, and also a way to denigrate the other side as weak on "republican" principles. In other words, from the Democratic-Republican perspective, the Federalists represented "bad" republicanism, or republicanism that stunk too much of monarchy and tyranny. "We're the real republicans," they were saying.

James Madison and Thomas Jefferson were the founders of this opposition movement against the Federalist agenda of Hamilton and Adams, and Jefferson eventually became the public face of the party. Like Hamilton had done with his own group, Madison and

Jefferson used their positions and influence to build a network of supporters throughout the country, finding especially strong support in the rural South and West.

As representatives of an opposition movement against the Federalist-controlled Congress (and later, presidency), the Democratic-Republican faction took opposing views on virtually every major issue supported by the Federalists.

Where the Federalists supported a strong, centralized federal government with a standing army, the Democratic-Republicans were the party of "states' rights," preferring state militias and arguing that the Federalists were putting too much power in the hands of the national government. They saw this federal power coming at the expense of the sovereignty of the individual states (a theme that has continued to be played out in American politics ever since).

Where the Federalists believed that industry and manufacturing were the ingredients of a strong economy, the Democratic-Republicans believed that promoting agriculture was a better way to build economic strength and pay off debt.

Where the Federalists saw America's greatness realized in building cities and expanding urban areas, the Democratic-Republicans believed that America's greatness lay in its frontier regions and opportunities for unlimited westward expansion.

And finally, where the Federalists were friendly with Great Britain and its king, and increasingly hostile towards the new republican government of France, the Democratic-Republicans were staunch supporters of the French and saw the Federalist treaties with Great Britain as more evidence of their weak adherence to republican principles.

In regards to these overwhelming fears of a Federalist descent into absolutism, Thomas Jefferson stated quite explicitly in a 1792 letter to George Washington: "The ultimate object of [the Federalist platform under Hamilton] is to prepare the way for a change, from the present form of republican government, to that of a monarchy."

As the opposition party, the Democratic-Republicans represented the minority view in Philadelphia during the 1790s (Philadelphia being, at that time, the seat of the federal government). In the same 1792 letter to George Washington, Jefferson said: "The republican party...are fewer in number [than the Federalist group]. They are fewer even when joined by the two, three, or half-dozen anti-federalists."

The "anti-federalists" Jefferson refers to are those statesmen, such as Virginia's Patrick Henry, who had been opposed to the ratification of the Constitution a few years earlier. Jefferson points out that although these people were opposed, in principle, to the entire system under which the country was now operating, they were more inclined to support Jefferson and the Democratic-Republicans than Hamilton and the Federalists. Even with their support, however, Jefferson's group represented a distinct minority.

This minority position for Jefferson's party was illustrated in the presidential election of 1796, where John Adams, representing the Federalists, defeated Thomas Jefferson, representing the Democratic-Republicans. However, the fact that Jefferson's party was gaining steam was also illustrated in this election: Jefferson only lost to Adams by three electoral votes, winning every state in the South and even taking Pennsylvania.

As we saw in the last chapter, the tide finally turned in favor of Jefferson's party when Adams and the Federalists provoked a war with France, then passed the Alien and Sedition Acts — legislation which to this day is among the most controversial ever passed by Congress.

With Jefferson's victory in the very contentious presidential election of 1800, the Democratic-Republican agenda became dominant. It remained in place, increasingly unopposed, through a succession of Democratic-Republican presidents and congresses, for the next two decades. It culminated in a period of relative peace and prosperity dubbed by historians "The Era of Good Feelings."

This period spans roughly from 1816 to 1824, coinciding with the presidency of James Monroe. If there has ever been a time in American history when the United States has functioned as a virtual one-party system, it was during this time.

By 1816, the Federalist numbers in Congress had dwindled to just a handful of mostly northeastern politicians, and the agrarian, states' rights agenda of Jefferson's party became the system — the norm — under which the country operated. Partisan bickering came to a virtual standstill, and (as we saw in the previous chapter) Monroe was re-elected in 1820 unopposed. The general feeling among the people was that the time for political parties was over; competing factions had been necessary in past decades, as the new country struggled to find its identity, but now those days were over and unity was the prescription for the future.

Unfortunately, those "good feelings" didn't last.

Monroe retired from the presidency in 1824, and four newcomers ran for president in a non-partisan race: Senator Andrew Jackson, Speaker of the House Henry Clay, Secretary of State John Quincy Adams, and Treasury Secretary William H. Crawford. Each of these candidates had support in certain regions of the country, with Jackson having the most widespread support due to his fame as a general. The election ultimately resulted in a dead-heat: all four candidates won multiple states and dozens of electoral votes, but none won a clear majority. Jackson had more electoral votes than any of the others, but it was still not enough to give him the presidency (the Constitution requires the winning candidate to have a majority of the overall electoral vote – Jackson came up 32 votes short). As a result, the election went to the House of Representatives, as mandated by the 12th Amendment. Since Henry Clay had won the fewest electoral votes of the four candidates, he was not eligible for the run-off election in the House. Instead, he used his position as Speaker of the House to influence the votes for the remaining three candidates. Clay's own economic philosophy was similar to that of John Quincy Adams, and Clay himself disliked Andrew Jackson and considered him unfit to be president. He would later say, in a speech to Congress:

> If [Jackson's brain] could be surveyed by Doctor Caldwell, of Transylvania University, I am persuaded that he would find the organ of destruction prominently developed.

Intent on keeping Jackson out of the White House, Clay was able to convince a significant number of congressmen that Adams was the best man for the job. Adams, in turn, promised Clay a prominent position in his cabinet if Clay succeeded in getting him elected.

Clay succeeded.

John Quincy Adams was elected president on the first ballot in the run-off election, and he promptly appointed Clay his Secretary of State, which was viewed by many as effectively naming Clay his successor, as three previous Secretaries (including Adams himself) had later become president.

Jackson, as one may imagine, was outraged, having fully expected to win the run-off, given his plurality in the general election of both popular votes and electoral votes. He accused Clay and Adams of corruption and backroom dealing (which was true), and spent the next four years strengthening his support around the country and painting the Adams-Clay faction as tyrannical and illegitimate.

The result of all this was, of course, an end to the non-partisan "Era of Good Feelings," and a descent back into factional, and eventually full-blown partisan, politics.

By the Numbers:

The Democratic-Republican Party

Founded: circa 1791

Period of Activity: About 35 years

Party Slogans: "Friends of Peace Will Vote for Jefferson;" "Monroe is the Man"

Number of Presidents: 4 (Thomas Jefferson, James Madison, James Monroe, John Quincy Adams)

Leading Party Figures: Thomas Jefferson, James Madison, George Clinton (Governor of New York and Vice-President under Jefferson), Albert Gallatin (Treasury Secretary under three presidents)

Main Platforms: States' rights, frontier expansion, republicanism, isolationism, civil liberties, support of agriculture over industry

THE 19th CENTURY DEMOCRATIC PARTY

THE DEMOCRATIC Party was founded by Andrew Jackson and his supporters in the late 1820s and early 1830s. It was born out of the rift that occurred during the 1824 presidential election, which resulted in the rise of new political factions after nearly a decade with very little partisan activity.

Future president Martin Van Buren, who was then a U.S. Senator from New York, helped to spearhead the new movement under Jackson, rallying support in the North for the southern general and war hero and his brand of states' rights politics. Like many in the now defunct Democratic-Republican Party, the Jacksonian Democrats believed strongly in westward expansion and a farm-based economy. In opposition, they were united in their general distrust of a powerful federal government, national banks, and urban elites. According to Princeton University historian Sean Wilentz, the party's numbers included strong support from farmers, urban laborers, and the socially-marginalized Irish Catholics. In short, the Democratic Party represented the concerns and ideologies of the common man.

With Van Buren solidifying votes in the North, Jackson ran for president again in 1828 and defeated incumbent John Quincy Adams, who Jackson viewed as having essentially stolen the election from him four years earlier. The Jackson faction became a full-blown political party during his time in the White House, and he rewarded Van Buren's efforts by making him Secretary of State. Van Buren would go on to follow Jackson to the presidency eight years later.

Under Jackson and later Van Buren, the Democrats waged war against the Second Bank of the United States, which had replaced Alexander Hamilton's First Bank after its charter expired. The Democrats viewed the national bank as little more than an economic oligarchy, with the federal government as its largest shareholder, and the greater part of the remaining stocks held by just a few hundred wealthy Americans and Europeans. For these early Democrats, this gave far too much economic power to the federal government and a few individuals, and did so at the expense of state sovereignty and the common man.

Jackson's battle paid off: the bank's charter failed to be renewed in the early 1830s, and it went private in 1836, shortly after Van Buren was elected to the White House. It was liquidated entirely by 1841. No central bank would exist again until the Federal Reserve was created in 1913.

The Democratic Party grew in numbers and strength over the next few decades. Between 1828 and 1860, Democrats lost only two presidential elections and maintained a majority in the House and/or the Senate in every year except the period of 1841-1843. During that virtual Golden Age spanning over thirty years, the Democrats controlled the presidency and *both* chambers of Congress for a total of sixteen (non-consecutive) years.

In time, however, party unity began to splinter. During the 1850s, a new breed of Democrats began bursting onto the scene in what has been referred to by historians as the "Young America" movement. Like the Tea Party movement within the Republican Party today, the Young America movement represented an enormously influential faction within the mainstream Democratic Party. Led by young, charismatic politicians like Stephen Douglas and future president Franklin Pierce, the faction moved away from the traditional agrarian politics of the Jacksonian, and embraced issues like commerce, technology, and internationalism. They promoted local jobs and infrastructure like bridges, railroads, and canals, and they were strong believers in American art and literature, supported by noted writers like Herman Melville and Nathaniel Hawthorne (Hawthorne actually wrote a biography of Franklin Pierce, published during Pierce's presidential campaign in 1852). Embracing the notion of American Exceptionalism, Young Americans supported a policy of Manifest Destiny, an ideology which affirmed that it was America's right and responsibility not only to settle the west and expand its own territories, but to export its culture and values to other countries.

At the same time that the Young America movement was revolutionizing the Democratic Party in the 1850s, the issue of slavery was beginning to drive a wedge not just between Democrats, but between all Americans from across the political spectrum. Young Americans, being primarily Northern Democrats, sought ways to avoid war with the South and permit slavery to die out on its own, while Southern Democrats made the expansion of slavery into new territories their top priority. Democratic legislation during this time attempted to solve the slavery question with the platform of Popular Sovereignty. Popular Sovereignty was the notion that new territories, when forming their own governments and applying for statehood, had the sovereign right to decide for themselves whether to permit slavery. This fit in perfectly with the long-held Democratic belief in states' rights.

The Kansas-Nebraska Act of 1854 was the centerpiece of the Popular Sovereignty ideology, overturning the Missouri Compromise of 1820, which had banned slavery in territories north of a specific latitude (essentially, a line drawn west from the southern border of Missouri, with slavery outlawed north of that line, and permitted south of it; there will be more on this law in later chapters). Instead, the Kansas-Nebraska Act permitted Kansas and Nebraska (which were both north of the old compromise line) to determine for themselves whether slavery would be permitted. The result was a minor civil war in the Kansas territory as pro-slavery and anti-slavery settlers flocked to the region in order to influence the outcome when the territory eventually applied for statehood.

By the time the 1860 presidential election rolled around, the Democratic Party was essentially split between North and South. In the end, the Northern Democrats nominated their own candidate for the presidency, while the Southern Democrats chose someone else. A third faction of Democrats – mostly from border states and with the sole purpose of preserving the Union – nominated a third man for the White House. With the Democrats thus split, Republican Abraham Lincoln coasted to victory, the South seceded and formed the Confederate States of America, and war became inevitable.

Following the outbreak of hostilities, the Northern Democrats split into two camps: the War Democrats, who supported Lincoln's military policies to put the Union back together, and the so-called Copperheads – anti-war Democrats who were content to let the South go and instead called for peace talks with the Confederacy.

Once the war was over, the Democratic Party became little more than a minor opposition party in Washington.

During this turbulent time in American history, many political parties and factions collapsed completely, but the Democratic Party managed to weather the storm. Its Golden Age, however, was over for good, and it would be decades before the party would completely recover from the scourge of the Civil War and the Reconstruction Era.

After 1856, only one Democrat won the presidency for the remaining 44 years of the century: Grover Cleveland, who served two non-consecutive terms (he lost his first bid for re-election in 1888, but won again in 1892). Prior to Cleveland's initial victory in 1884, no Democrat had held the White House in nearly 25 years. Even after Cleveland helped get the party back into national prominence, it would still be well into the 20th century before the party fully recovered from its association with slavery and, later, segregation.

In the last few decades of the 19th century, the Democratic Party became associated with policies that, in previous years, they had fought against. Led by the likes of Cleveland, they supported capitalism and banking, promoted lower tariffs to encourage international trade, and fought for Civil Service reform in order to break the century-old patronage system that had led to waste, cronyism, and corruption in government (this patronage system had been championed by the first Democrat, Andrew Jackson). They continued, however, to bill themselves as the party of the common man, supporting labor unions, rural interests, some regulation of business, and infrastructure. They were also strongly opposed to imperialism: Democrats heavily criticized America's imperialist tendencies during and after the Spanish-American War (which occurred in 1898) as essentially un-American and monarchical.

Splits still occurred, however, and this is no doubt one reason why the party frequently failed to win federal elections. Not only did the party remain split geographically between rural Southerners who supported segregation, and urban Northerners who did not, but the party frequently split over economic issues as well. Most notably, liberal Democrats, led by William Jennings Bryan, split from conservative Democrats led by Grover Cleveland, over the issue of the gold standard in the 1890s. The gold standard essentially valued American currency based on its equivalent in gold. Cleveland supported the gold standard because it encouraged international trade with foreign countries who were also on the gold standard (thus, the gold standard brought more revenue into the federal coffers and helped keep prices stable). In contrast, Jennings and other so-called "bimetallists" argued that the gold standard hindered the domestic economy because it caused silver, which was more abundant, to lose its value. Instead, they sought to alter America's currency by introducing silver into the equation and making it legal tender together with gold (hence the moniker "bimetallism"). Eventually, the Bryan faction lost this fight: the gold standard, an unwritten rule throughout most of the 19th century, became official government policy in the early 20th century.

In any case, these factional and regional disputes characterized the Democratic Party throughout the last few decades of the 19th century, and helped ensure that they remained, by and large, the minority party in Washington politics.

By the Numbers:

The Democratic Party of the 19th Century

Founded: circa 1828

Period of Activity: Ongoing

Party Slogans: "Jackson, Calhoun, and Liberty" (1828); "We Polked You in '44, We Shall Pierce You in '52" (1852); "Peace, Union, and Constitutional Government" (1868); "A Public Office is a Public Trust" (1892)

Number of Presidents: 6 (Andrew Jackson, Martin Van Buren, James K. Polk, Franklin Pierce, James Buchanan, Grover Cleveland)

(Some lists include a 7th Democrat in Andrew Johnson, but he had been elected vice-president with Abraham Lincoln in 1864 on a fusion ticket and was not an active member of either party during his presidency.)

Leading Party Figures: Andrew Jackson, Martin Van Buren, Stephen Douglas, John C. Breckenridge (Vice-President under James Buchanan, presidential candidate for the Southern Democrats in 1860), Samuel J. Tilden (governor of New York, won the popular vote for president in 1876 but lost the electoral vote), Grover Cleveland, William Jennings Bryan

Main Platforms: States' rights, frontier expansion, opposition to abolition, Manifest Destiny, Popular Sovereignty, rights of the common American, agrarianism, low tariffs, big business (especially later in the century)

THE NATIONAL REPUBLICAN PARTY

NOT TO BE confused with the later Republican Party, the National Republican Party began as a faction surrounding John Quincy Adams, following his controversial presidential victory in 1824. Made up primarily of former Federalists and other like-minded people, the National Republicans came to be led by Adams' Secretary of State Henry Clay.

As we saw earlier, as Speaker of the House in 1824, Clay was instrumental in securing a victory for Adams in the House run-off election, and thereby secured the devotion of the Adams men, and the enmity of the Jacksonians.

Following Adams' resounding defeat in 1828, Clay's party became an opposition party, fighting continually against the states' rights policies of Andrew Jackson and the Democrats. The term "National Republican" seems to have been coined around 1830.

One of the centerpieces of the National Republican platform was an economic policy championed by Clay and dubbed the "American System." Based on the philosophy and ideology of Alexander Hamilton's system from the 1790s, the American System promoted government subsidies to finance infrastructure and internal improvements, such as roads and bridges and canals, in order to ease travel and, especially, open trade routes among cities and states, thereby stimulating the national economy. To pay for this and other programs, there would be a protective tariff – a high tax on foreign products entering the United States. This tariff would not only help pay for internal improvements, but would also encourage domestic manufacturing by reducing the overall amount of foreign goods (i.e. "competition") in the market. Finally, the National Republicans supported the federal banking system as a means of stabilizing currency and, ultimately, strengthening the American economy.

We have already seen how the Democrats, led by Jackson, fought successfully to privatize the federal banking system, and it was Clay and his coalition of National Republicans who had fought to keep it in place. Clay was, by this time, a U.S. Senator, and under his direction, Congress passed a bill in 1832 extending the charter of the Second National Bank (which was due to expire in four years). Jackson vetoed it and Clay led an attempt to override the veto, but it failed.

The Democrats also fought endlessly over other provisions in Clay's American System, particularly the protective tariffs. In 1828, South Carolina threatened to secede over the issue, and began refusing to enforce the federal tariff at its own harbors and dockyards, feeling that the tax would damage its economy, which depended on many foreign goods. Despite being opposed in principle to high tariffs, Jackson threatened to personally lead the armies into South Carolina to enforce federal laws, and Clay eventually worked out a deal in Congress to lower the tariff to more agreeable levels.

Always skeptical of "big government," the Democrats also fought the National Republicans over their policy of internal improvements, with Jackson vetoing a bill in 1830 that would have permitted the federal government to purchase several road-building companies.

Prior to 1828, presidents had generally been nominated by congressional caucuses – groups of like-minded congressmen who would gather and nominate one of their own for president. That system broke down after the debacle of the 1824 election, and in 1828, the two candidates were nominated by state factions. By the time the 1832 election rolled around, the idea of a nominating convention had been born, and the National Republicans were one of the first parties to hold one.

Nominating Henry Clay, the National Republicans made the federal bank crisis the centerpiece of their campaign, attacking Jackson for vetoing the renewal of the bank's charter, and depicting him as a tyrant intent on abusing the balance of powers in Washington. This issue of the president's veto power, and what constituted a fair use of it, would become a central theme in national politics for several decades to come. It was born largely out of the National Republican perspective that Jackson had misused the power by overruling legitimate Congressional legislation. If Congress represented the "will of the people," then vetoing a piece of legislation was tantamount to acting like a king. For his part, Jackson vetoed twelve different pieces of legislation during his two terms as president – more than all previous presidents combined.

During the 1832 election, political cartoons in favor of Clay frequently played on this theme. One famous cartoon shows Jackson in the traditional garb of the British king, holding a scepter in one hand, a scroll labeled "Veto" in the other, and standing atop a U.S. Constitution that has been torn to pieces. The caption reads: "Born to Command. King Andrew the First."

Despite the attacks, Jackson won re-election in a landslide. Clay won only six states, and just 37% of the popular vote. Following this defeat, the coalition of National Republicans around Henry Clay collapsed, and its members and ideologues migrated into new factions and parties that were beginning to emerge by the middle of Jackson's second term.

By the Numbers:

The National Republican Party

Founded: circa 1825

Period of Activity: About ten years

Party Slogans: "The Spirit of Jacksonianism is Jacobinism;" "King Andrew"

Number of Presidents: 0 (John Quincy Adams was elected president in 1824 as a Democratic-Republican; however, the National Republican Party formed initially as a faction supporting Adams, and they nominated him for re-election in 1828. He lost that election, however, so he cannot be called a true National Republican president.)

Leading Party Figures: Henry Clay, John Quincy Adams, John Sergeant (Pennsylvania Congressman, running mate to Henry Clay in 1832)

Main Platforms: Federally-backed internal improvements, federal banks, business and industry, protective tariffs

THE ANTI-MASONIC PARTY

THE ANTI-MASONIC Party is widely-considered the first true "third party" in American political history. Arising around the same time as the National Republican Party in the late 1820s, it was (as the name implies) initially a one-issue party: opposition to Freemasonry. Specifically, the members of this party were opposed to what they perceived as too much influence by secretive masonic ideology on the politics and economics of the United States.

They were, perhaps, the nation's first conspiracy theorists.

In late 1826, a New Yorker named William Morgan, who had apparently been denied admission into a Masonic Lodge in Batavia, New York, decided to publish an exposé about the Freemasons, divulging their secrets to the world. The Freemasons, as one might imagine, were none too happy about this, so in September of 1826, a few local members managed to have him arrested for stealing a shirt and tie. It very quickly became apparent, however, that these charges were baseless, and Morgan was released. Despite that, within just a few hours, Morgan was arrested again, this time being charged with failure to pay a debt (Anti-Masonic Party member Millard Fillmore would later lead a push in the New York General Assembly to abolish debtors' prisons). This time, Morgan was kept behind bars until later that night when an unidentified man came and paid the debt on Morgan's behalf. Morgan was then seen riding away in a carriage with this man and several others. They were seen the following morning near Fort Niagara, some sixty miles away at the Canadian border.

After that, Morgan was never seen again.

Morgan's disappearance caused a sensation throughout New York and the surrounding states, with the Freemasons being accused of abducting Morgan from his jail cell and threatening him until he fled the country. When a man's badly-desiccated body was found downriver from Fort Niagara about a year later, suspicions of kidnapping turned to suspicions of murder.

Anti-masonic furor erupted across New England, especially in New York where Freemasons were heavily involved in the political machine that ran the state government. The movement attracted many churches and religious denominations, with Freemasonry being likened to paganism and preachers encouraging their congregations not only to avoid Freemasonry in general, but especially to stop voting for politicians with ties to the group. The Freemasons in government were seen as a group of elitists who were collaborating to achieve the goals of the organization, and doing so at the expense of the common people and the Constitution.

Since many of these same Freemasons (particularly in New York) were joining and becoming supporters of the new Democratic Party of Andrew Jackson (who was also a Freemason), politicians opposed to their views and platforms began to use anti-masonic sentiment to gather support and rally voters.

What resulted was the first third party in American politics: The Anti-Masonic Party.

A number of Anti-Masonic candidates won state seats in New York in 1828, and by the early 1830s the movement had gone national. By this time, it began expanding its platforms to include internal improvements and high tariffs – making the party a friend of the National Republican movement. Sympathetic newspapers were used to spread the message of the Anti-Masons, with the primary one being the Albany Evening News, begun by printer and New York General Assembly member Thurlow Weed. This paper would remain in circulation until the 1920s, and at one point, during the 1840s, was the biggest political paper in the entire country.

In addition to being the nation's first true third party, the Anti-Masonic Party also invented the tradition of using conventions to nominate candidates for the presidency. As we saw in an earlier chapter, congressional caucuses had been responsible in the past for nominating men to the presidency; with the innovations of the Anti-Masonic Party, this was now done at the party level, where delegates elected locally would meet together in a national convention and choose a candidate of their liking. It would be decades before presidential primaries would become part of this process, but our modern tradition of nominating candidates at national party conventions can be traced directly to the Anti-Masonic Party of the early 1830s. They held their first nominating convention in September of 1831, and 96 delegates from among ten states nominated former Attorney General William Wirt for the 1832 presidential election.

Two months later, the National Republicans followed suit and held a convention of their own, followed in May of 1832 by the Democrats.

Jackson won re-election easily that year, but Wirt and the Anti-Masons took 7% of the popular vote and won the state of Vermont.

The Anti-Masonic Party began to disintegrate following the 1832 election, as many of its members began joining with former members of the National Republican Party to create a new party that brought in elements of both. However, a few states – namely Vermont and Pennsylvania – continued to have active Anti-Masonic Party systems for several more years, and both those states met in state-based conventions in 1836 to nominate William Henry Harrison for president. A national Anti-Masonic convention was also held that year, but the delegates ultimately chose not to nominate anyone.

The party lasted in remnants until at least 1838, when yet another national convention was held. At that time, the Anti-Masons again nominated William Henry Harrison for the 1840 presidency, but the party had essentially disappeared from existence by the time that election actually took place, and Harrison ran on a different ticket.

By the Numbers:

The Anti-Masonic Party

Founded: circa 1827

Period of Activity: About ten years

Party Slogans: "Time Cuts Down All, Both Great and Small"

Number of Presidents: 0 (The highest office held by any Anti-Masonic Party member was that of governor, in both Vermont and Pennsylvania)

Leading Party Figures: Thurlow Weed (New York politician, newspaperman, and political organizer), William H. Seward (New York politician who would eventually become Secretary of State under Abraham Lincoln), William Wirt, Millard Fillmore (New York politician, future U.S. president), Francis Granger (New York politician and party president)

Main Platforms: Ending the influence of Freemasonry over state and U.S. politics, internal improvements, protective tariffs

THE WHIG PARTY

THE WHIG Party was formed in the 1830s from the remnants of the National Republican Party and the Anti-Masonic Party, as well as non-affiliated opponents of Andrew Jackson. The first major party to present a serious threat to the powerful Democratic Party, the Whigs would eventually see four men serve in the presidency before slavery and factional disputes reduced the party to the pages of history.

As president, Andrew Jackson proved to be a major reformer. If you ever wonder why modern presidents have the powers and influence they have, and why they seem to be constantly at odds with Congress, trace it back to Andrew Jackson. Jackson was responsible for transforming the Executive Branch of the federal government from a largely hands-off position focused primarily on foreign policy, to a very powerful, centralized office with heavy influence in domestic and economic affairs.

Congress had always been viewed as the primary voice of the people; Jackson now brought this perspective to the presidency, believing the president, as leader of all citizens in all states, was more suited to this role than congressmen who only represented tiny regions of constituents. This friction between Jackson and Congress is illustrated in a statistic noted earlier: Jackson vetoed more Congressional legislation than all previous presidents combined.

Needless to say, this created a lot of backlash during his time in office, which is why so many political parties and factions in opposition to him began springing up during those years. Regardless of their political affiliation, his opponents saw him as domineering and viewed his actions and decisions as increasingly autocratic. As we saw in a previous chapter, he was routinely referred to by opponents as "King Andrew."

The Whig Party was the culmination of all the opposition that formed around Jackson's heavy-handed use of his presidential powers. Politically, the party was a kind of combination of the old Federalist and Democratic-Republican values. Like the Federalists of previous eras, Whigs embraced a strong, centralized economic system similar to the one championed by Alexander Hamilton and which sought to build up the cities and urban areas of the nation with government subsidies, paid for with high tariffs and revenues from the sale of federal lands, and all centered around a federal banking system. From the Democratic-Republicans of the early eras, they took a strong view of states' rights with limited power to Congress and, especially, the president.

Henry Clay and Massachusetts Senator Daniel Webster were the virtual founders of the Whig Party, and the name was chosen because the term "Whig" – derived from the anti-monarchy political party in England – referred to people who were opposed to tyranny. Many of the leaders of the American Revolution had referred to themselves as "Whigs" for the same reason, and the new party was undoubtedly trying to play on that spirit of national pride, revolution, patriotism, and core American values.

In the same way that the largely urban Federalists had been branded as aristocratic elitists by their rural foes, so too did the agrarian-minded Democrats of the 1840s and 50s accuse the Whigs of elitism and snobbery. For the most part, industrialists, bankers, and other economic professionals supported Whig politics, while Democrats appealed more to farmers, laborers, and common people. Democrats tended to be more successful in federal political elections, while Whigs – for a time, at least – came to dominate many state governments, particularly in the North.

By the time the election of 1836 had rolled around, the new Whig Party was ready to nominate its first man for the presidency. There was one minor problem, however: the party was still in its infancy, with several different factions separated not only on political issues but also by geography, and the party did not yet have a national organization. The result was that, for the only time in U.S. history outside of the Civil War era, a single political party nominated more than one person for president. In fact, the Whigs nominated *four* men for president that year.

Among Whigs in New England, Daniel Webster initially had the most support, but as the election drew nearer, war hero and Ohioan

William Henry Harrison began to take center stage. Meanwhile, in the South, Whig groups nominated Tennessee Senator Hugh Lawson White for the presidency, while South Carolina Whigs opted for North Carolina Senator Willie Person Mangum. The result was that most of the northern states had Harrison on the ballot, and most southern states had White, but South Carolina's ballot had Mangum, while the ballot in Massachusetts had Webster.

With their ticket split four ways, the Whigs knew they had no hope of gaining the required majority of electoral votes. However, their strategy was to split the vote among their candidates and the Democrat, Martin Van Buren, causing no one to receive a majority, and the election sent to the House of Representatives – which is what had happened in 1824. The House, in 1836, had a Democratic majority (139-102), so the hope was that Van Buren would receive the lowest number of electoral votes and thus not be eligible for the House run-off.

The strategy failed miserably. All five candidates did end up winning electoral votes, but Van Buren still managed to win a clear majority (he needed 148 and received 170). In an unusual turn of events, his running mate, Richard Mentor Johnson of Kentucky, only received 147 electoral votes (all the electors from Virginia cast ballots for Van Buren, but refused, due to political differences, to vote for Johnson). As a result, no vice-president had a majority, so the election went to a run-off in the U.S. Senate, as mandated by the Constitution. Johnson won the run-off easily.

Despite losing the presidential election in 1836, the various Whig candidates won nearly half of the popular vote (Van Buren took 50.8%, with the rest going to the Whigs), and the party grew in numbers and organization very quickly after that.

One of the overarching ideologies embraced by many Whigs involved the presidential veto, which, as we saw in a previous chapter, had become a bone of contention during the veto-happy terms of Andrew Jackson. Whigs came to view the veto – particularly as Jackson had used it – as contrary to the values and ideals of the Founding Fathers. The veto, they insisted, should only be used when the president believed a piece of legislation was unconstitutional, or if there was a valid reason to believe that the legislation was sectional in nature – that is, enriching one region of the country while bankrupting another. Otherwise, vetoing perfectly valid legislation was tantamount to tyranny. Jackson had used the veto to kill bills he didn't agree with – bills that were contrary to his own political vision for America. This is something, of course, that continues right up to the present day. Whigs saw this as an abuse of power that threatened to upset the delicate balance between the Executive and Legislative branches of government.

William Henry Harrison, during his inauguration speech in 1841, summed up the Whig perspective:

> [The power of the veto] in the hands of one individual would seem to be an incongruity in our system. I consider the veto power [to be] a conservative power…to be used only first, to protect the Constitution …secondly, the people from the effects of hasty legislation where their will has been disregarded…and thirdly, [to protect] the rights of minorities.

After coming in second in the 1836 election to Martin Van Buren, Harrison (running as the only Whig candidate) won the 1840 rematch in a landslide, thanks largely to an economic recession during Van Buren's presidency. That same recession hurt Congress too: in addition to winning their first presidency, Whigs also won a majority in both congressional chambers.

The good times, however, were not destined to last. Harrison's presidency became the shortest in history when he died of pneumonia just one month into his term. His vice-president, John Tyler, ascended to the White House.

Tyler was a former Democrat who had only joined the Whigs after breaking with Jackson over the issue of states' rights as they pertained to a state's power to overrule a federal law. This had become a serious issue in the 1830s (known to history as the Nullification Crisis), and led to a lot of moderate Democrats (who supported nullification) defecting to the new Whig coalition. As a result, Tyler's political allegiances were somewhat dubious to the newly-elected Whig leaders of Congress, and it wasn't long before everything broke down.

Senator Henry Clay, who was the most public and powerful face of the Whig Party, introduced a bill to reestablish the national bank that Andrew Jackson had done away with. Tyler vetoed it, and when they rewrote the bill in an effort to overcome Tyler's objections, he vetoed it again.

Recall that, for many Whigs, the veto was only to be used in extraordinary circumstances and only if a bill was deemed unconstitutional or in some way discriminatory. Also recall that an economically strong federal government, backed by a national bank, was one of the hallmarks of Whig politics.

Needless to say, the Whigs in Congress were furious. Following his second veto, in September of 1841, all but one of his cabinet members resigned in protest, hoping to force Tyler himself to resign. After a few days, when it became apparent that Tyler would not resign, the congressional Whigs expelled him from the party. Tyler, in effect, became an Independent for the rest of his presidency.

Throughout the remainder of the 1840s, the Whigs continued to remain a force in Washington politics, but their internal struggles with Tyler gave new momentum to the Democrats, who began winning majorities in Congress again, and also defeated Henry Clay in 1844 to put James K. Polk in the White House. The annexation of Texas, and subsequent war with Mexico, became a major issue in the last half of the decade, with the Whigs initially opposing it (including Whig congressman Abraham Lincoln), but later switching tactics after nominating Mexican-American War hero Zachary Taylor for the presidency in 1848.

Taylor won the election, but, like Tyler before him, proved to be a thorn in the side for Whigs in Washington. Taylor was a political outsider and career military man who had never been involved in politics. Prior to his own election, it was widely reported that he had never even voted in a presidential election. Though he supported typical Whig platforms like the primacy of Congress in legislative matters, vetoes to be used only to protect the Constitution, and government assistance for manufacturing and industry, he differed from many Whigs on tariffs and banking. According to historian Michael F. Holt of the University of Virginia, Taylor was publically indifferent to many cherished Whig beliefs, but made private statements expressing cynical views on Whig policies; Holt states that Taylor, effectively, "pronounced an epitaph for the entire Whig economic program."

Like the first general-turned-politician that the Whigs managed to elect to the White House (Harrison), Taylor also died in office and was succeeded by his vice-president, former Anti-Mason Millard Fillmore. Unlike his predecessor, Fillmore held staunch Whig views and worked together with his comrades in Congress to pass the Compromise of 1850, which avoided a secession crisis and seemed, for a time, to put off the increasingly virulent problem of slavery and its expansion into new territories (more on this in the next chapter).

The slavery issue, however, was far from gone, and as the 1850s progressed, it fractured the Whig Party across northern and southern lines. The anti-slavery northern Whigs managed to block Fillmore's nomination for president in 1852, causing the party to fall back on yet another war hero, Winfield Scott. The third time was not a charm for the Whigs, and Scott lost in a landslide. Whigs had not controlled either branch of Congress since 1849, and would, in fact, never win a majority again. In that same year of 1852, Henry Clay and Daniel Webster, two of the most prominent and powerful members of the party, both died, creating a vacuum of leadership and effectively destroying the heart and soul of the party.

By 1856, with many Whigs throughout the country defecting to new parties or leaving politics all together (as Abraham Lincoln did for a time), the Whigs held their last convention. Rather than nominating their own ticket, they simply voted to support the ticket of the new American Party, which had already nominated Millard Fillmore. After that final act, the party essentially disbanded.

Despite its ultimate failure, the Whig Party made several lasting contributions to the American political system, and many of its platforms and ideologies were absorbed into both the Democratic and Republican parties in later decades. Indeed, the Whig notion of government funding for internal improvements has continued right up to the present day.

One of the Whig Party's most lasting contributions to the United States was the development of the public school system. Whig politician Horace Mann, who served in both the Massachusetts legislature and the U.S. Congress, together with fellow Connecticut Whig Henry Barnard, enacted numerous educational reforms in their respective states that would eventually spread across the nation, including the notion that public education should be required for all children and paid for through taxation. Unlike many Democrats of the time, Whigs believed strongly in the power of education, believing it held the key to American economic strength. Though it would be decades before this vision would come to fruition, the Whig perspective on education still underpins many of our educational policies today.

By the Numbers:

The Whig Party

Founded: circa 1834

Period of Activity: About twenty years

Party Slogans: "Equal and Full Protection to American Industry" (1836); "Tippecanoe and Tyler Too" (1840); "General Taylor Never Surrenders" (1848); "Protection to American Labor" (1852)

Number of Presidents: 4 (William Henry Harrison, John Tyler [expelled from party during presidency], Zachary Taylor, Millard Fillmore)

Leading Party Figures: Henry Clay, Daniel Webster, William Henry Harrison, Horace Greeley (editor for the Whig newspaper *New York Tribune*), John Quincy Adams (after his 1820s presidency, he served in Congress as a Whig), Abraham Lincoln (leader of the Whig Party in Illinois), Willie Person Mangum (U.S. Senator from North Carolina and one of the founders of the party)

Main Platforms: Protective tariffs, internal improvements and infrastructure, less centralized Executive Branch with limited veto power, national banks, education reform

THE LIBERTY PARTY AND THE FREE SOIL PARTY

LIKE THE Anti-Masonic Party of the previous decade, the Liberty Party was formed in 1839 as a single-issue party advocating a complete abolition of slavery – the first significant political party to do so.

Founded in New York, the party met in 1840 and nominated former Kentucky politician, lawyer, and abolitionist James G. Birney for the presidency. He received only a few thousand votes in that election, but when he was nominated again in 1844, he managed to take over 60,000 votes nationwide. In New York alone, he garnered some 16,000 votes. Democrat James K. Polk won New York over Whig Henry Clay in that election by just 5,000 votes. Had Clay won New York, he'd have won the election. Since most of the votes that went to Birney would likely have gone to Clay if Birney hadn't been in the race, Birney became the first third-party candidate to spoil an election for a major party candidate. (Birney also took about 2.3% of the popular vote; Polk only defeated Clay in the popular vote by 1.4%.)

The party was noted for its fiery anti-slavery rhetoric backed up with moralistic religious perspectives (in addition to opposing slavery, the party eventually began to call for the abolition of "sin" industries like alcohol, gambling, and prostitution, and thus became one of the forerunners of the later Prohibition Movement).

As voices in the party grew more extreme, moderate party members began to realize that if not for their fierce, religiously-backed abolitionist stance, they might be able to attract more members, and ultimately more voters. They realized that many northern voters were essentially anti-slavery, but did not feel comfortable with the controversial and moralistic "abolitionist" title.

As a result, in 1848, the moderates of the party met with disaffected anti-slavery members of the New York Democratic Party and joined together under a new party and new brand: the Free Soil

Party. The more radical elements of the Liberty Party continued for several years afterward, but they played little to no role in major politics.

Before delving into the ideologies of the Free Soil Party, it is important to understand the American political landscape during this period.

In the late 1840s and early 1850s, the territorial expansion of slavery became a prominent issue in American politics. More and more pioneers were moving westward and settling lands in the newly acquired territories ceded from Mexico at the end of the Mexican-American War in 1848. These territories included virtually all of the modern states of Arizona, Utah, Nevada, and California, as well as portions of Colorado, New Mexico, and Wyoming.

The Missouri Compromise of 1820 had made the expansion of slavery illegal anywhere north of the Arkansas-Missouri border (with Missouri, itself, being excepted). At that time, the law had only applied to the newly acquired Louisiana Purchase, which included all of the Great Plains territory up to the Canadian border (the modern states of Oklahoma, Kansas, Nebraska, the Dakotas, Montana, etc.). When Texas was annexed in 1845, however, the Missouri Compromise line was extended westward to the western edge of the Texas Panhandle, thereby permitting slavery in Texas.

When the U.S. won all the territory west of Texas at the end of the Mexican-American War, a dispute arose as to whether the Missouri Compromise Line would continue to extend westward all the way to California – thus outlawing slavery north of the line, and permitting it to the south – or whether the line would remain where it was (ending at the Texas Panhandle, leaving the status of the new territory up in the air).

In 1850, following the death of President Zachary Taylor (who was staunchly against it), a new compromise was passed by Congress that addressed these issues. Spearheaded by Whig luminary Henry Clay, there were several important facets to this Compromise of 1850:

1. California would become the 31st state and would not have slaves. A proposal by pro-slavery politicians to split California, and thus allow the southern portion to adopt slavery, was defeated.
2. Two new territories would be organized – the New Mexico territory (comprising modern day New Mexico and Arizona) and the Utah territory (comprising modern day Utah and Nevada). Both these territories would be open for settlement, and any eventual state formed from these territories would be permitted to become slave states if the citizens approved it. Southern lawmakers had hoped to make the uninhabited areas of the New Mexico territory a third territory where slavery might more easily expand, but this was defeated. Northern lawmakers had hoped to extend the boundary of the Missouri Compromise Line to effectively prohibit slavery in the northern areas of the new territory, but this too was defeated.
3. The so-called Wilmot Proviso, which had sought to outlaw slavery in all the territory ceded by Mexico, was defeated.
4. A new Fugitive Slave Law was enacted, requiring any escaped slave to be returned to his owner.

This compromise helped to ease tension, for a few years at least, over the issue of how slavery would, or would not, be expanded into new U.S. territories.

The Free Soil Party sprang from the ashes of the Liberty Party right as these territorial issues began flaring up at the end of the Mexican-American War in 1848. The party was, in effect, a kinder, gentler Liberty Party. Instead of dishing out fierce, controversial rhetoric calling for the complete prohibition of slavery, they developed a platform aimed at subtly squeezing slavery out of existence through attrition. They effectively skirted the moral issues of slavery, and instead argued that the U.S. economy did not need slavery to thrive. Free men, working their own land on small farms, were better-suited to strengthen the U.S. economy than slaves working on enormous plantations owned by a single person. This ideology was put into practice by their support of the failed Wilmot Proviso, and, later, in their push to grant western lands to so-called "homesteaders," thereby denying those new territories to large plantation owners who would bring crews of slaves with them.

The idea of the homesteader had been created by an 1841 law that permitted independent farmers in U.S. territories ("squatters") to purchase their land from the federal government for very low costs, before the land went up for public sale. The Free Soil Party pushed for a revision of this law which would permit these squatters to receive their land for no cost at all from the federal government (thus, "free soil"). Doing so, they believed, would encourage more and more small farmers (who, by and large, did not own slaves) to settle new lands in the west. The idea was to populate the new western territories with folks who were not married to the institution of slavery, and who would, in turn, ensure that any new state formed from those territories did not enter the Union as a slave state. Pushing for farmers to be given land for free, of course, put them at odds with the Whigs, whose economic policy was based, in part, on earning revenue from the sale of federal lands.

The Free Soil Party's first presidential ticket was, in today's parlance, a true "rock star" ticket: in 1848, they nominated former Democratic president Martin Van Buren for the presidency with Charles Francis Adams – son and grandson of former presidents – as his running mate. Though the ticket did not win any electoral votes, Van Buren and Adams did win 10% of the overall popular vote, most of which came from anti-slavery Democrats. The result was that the Whig candidate, Zachary Taylor (who was also opposed to the expansion of slavery), was able to defeat Democrat Lewis Cass.

The Compromise of 1850 put a damper on the continued growth of the Free Soil Party. The party had been founded on issues related to the expansion of slavery, and with that question (at least temporarily) put to rest, many anti-slavery Democrats who had flocked to the Free Soil Party in 1848 began to return to the Democratic fold. The failure of the Wilmot Proviso, which had been primarily supported by Free Soilers, also caused disenchantment within the young party's ranks.

The result was that in 1852, with prominent abolitionist and New Hampshire Senator John Parker Hail on the ticket, the party won less than 5% of the popular vote – a drop of more than 50% from their support in 1848. Democrat Franklin Pierce won in a landslide.

Following the failure of the Free Soil effort to ban slavery in new territories, the party turned to the aforementioned policy of supporting homesteaders – offering federal lands to independent farmers in the new territories, hoping to populate the territories with enough anti-slavery elements to defeat any attempts at establishing legalized slavery there.

This ideology came to a head in 1854 after the passage of the Kansas-Nebraska Act. Recall that the Missouri Compromise of 1820 had outlawed slavery in the Louisiana Purchase north of the Arkansas-Missouri border. By 1854, this included all the unorganized territory north of Texas, through the heartland of the American continent.

The Kansas-Nebraska Act effectively repealed the Missouri Compromise. It permitted slavery to expand to the newly organized territories of Kansas and Nebraska, both of which had been north of the Missouri Compromise Line. The law was based, as we saw previously, on the Democratic Party's principle of Popular Sovereignty, championed by Illinois Senator Stephen Douglas, which sought to permit new settlers to choose for themselves whether to organize a state with slavery or without slavery. This notion had played a role in the Compromise of 1850 as well, but that law had only impacted the new western territory ceded from Mexico, not the unorganized territory of the old Louisiana Purchase.

Free Soilers and other anti-slavery advocates were outraged.

As we noted previously, a minor civil war broke out in the Kansas territory (hence the nickname "Bleeding Kansas") as anti-slavery settlers and pro-slavery settlers raced to buy up the land, hoping to get enough like-minded individuals in the territory to affect the eventual passage, or prohibition, of slavery. The anti-slavery folks in Kansas were called Jayhawkers, while their pro-slavery opponents were called Border Ruffians (because they frequently came across the border from Missouri to encourage pro-slavery votes and scare off potential Jayhawk voters).

Although the Free Soil Party is often lauded for its early opposition to the expansion of slavery, the party's biggest failing was its motivation for opposition. While some Free Soilers were adamant abolitionists, the party itself took an ambivalent stance on the morality of slavery, and many Free Soilers were, by any modern definition, staunch racists. They pushed for "free soil and free labor" not because they were united in a belief that slavery was immoral, but because they wanted to keep black slave labor from effectively limiting the ability of white people to own and farm their own land in new states. David Wilmot, the Pennsylvania Senator who wrote the Wilmot Proviso, stated emphatically that he supported "the rights of white freemen," so that "free white labor" could inherit a "fair country...where the sons...of my own race and own color" could operate "without the disgrace [that] negro slavery brings upon free labor."

However, other elements of the Free Soil Party were more genuine in their concern for the plight of blacks, and pushed for an easing of so-called "Black Laws" in many states. In Ohio, for instance, a set of laws had been enacted in 1807 to discourage freed slaves from settling in Ohio (and thus competing for jobs and land with whites). Among other things, people of color were required to show a certificate proving they were free before they would be allowed to settle in the state, and they were also required to find two white people who would put up $500 in surety guaranteeing the applicant's "good behavior." Ohio's Free Soil legislators successfully lobbied for these laws to be overturned in 1849.

One legacy that outlasted the party itself was their support of homesteaders. In 1861, after the southern states had seceded (and thus no longer had representatives in Congress to block the bill), the Homestead Act was passed, allowing people to apply for ownership, at absolutely no cost, for up to 160 acres of undeveloped land west of the Mississippi River. The law remained in effect until the 1970s.

Abolitionist remnants of the Free Soilers and Whigs met in Illinois following the passage of the controversial Kansas-Nebraska Act in 1854. United by their opposition to what they perceived as an advancement of the "slave power" ideology, and recognizing that both parties were falling apart by internal factions and disputes, they formed the nucleus of an organization that would eventually come to be known as the Grand Ol' Party.

By the Numbers:

The Liberty Party

Founded: circa 1840

Period of Activity: About twelve years

Party Slogans: "Slavery is Against Natural Rights"

Number of Presidents: 0 (the party nominated candidates in every election from 1840 to 1852, but only James G. Birney in 1844 ever managed to win more than 0.3% of the popular vote)

Leading Party Figures: James G. Birney, Salmon P. Chase (future governor of Ohio and later Chief Justice of the U.S. Supreme Court), William Goodell (prominent New York journalist, abolitionist, and author of the party's platform)

Main Platforms: Abolishment of slavery, religious morality

By the Numbers:

The Free Soil Party

Founded: 1848

Period of Activity: About six years

Party Slogans: "Free Soil, Free Speech, Free Labor, and Free Men"

Number of Presidents: 0 (candidates were nominated in 1848 and 1852 but neither won any electoral votes)

Leading Party Figures: Martin Van Buren, John P. Hale, Charles Francis Adams, William Cullen Bryant (renowned editor of the New York Evening Post), David Broderick (U.S. Senator from California and leader of the Free Soil Party there), Charles Sumner (U.S. Senator from Massachusetts and leading abolitionist, famously beaten nearly to death in the chambers of the U.S. Senate in 1856 because of an anti-slavery speech he gave)

Main Platforms: Opposition to slavery's expansion into U.S. territories, moderate tariffs to raise government revenue, subsidies on a limited basis for internal improvements, enactment of a homestead law

THE 19TH CENTURY REPUBLICAN PARTY

THE REPUBLICAN Party was founded in 1854 by a confluence of three important factors: the fracturing of the Whig Party, the floundering of the Free Soil Party, and the passage of the Kansas-Nebraska Act.

In the few years prior to 1854, the Whig Party had become fractured not just between anti-slavery northern Whigs and pro-slavery southern Whigs, but also among the northern Whigs themselves. On one side was the abolitionist faction of the northern party, sometimes called "Conscience Whigs," who made the moral depravity of slavery their central concern. On the other side were the so-called "Cotton Whigs," who frequently had financial interests in the southern states and who were, therefore, much more ambivalent about abolishing slavery all together. By 1854, these fractures, together with the deaths of prominent Whig leaders like Henry Clay and Daniel Webster, had left the party essentially defunct on a national level.

As we saw in the last chapter, the Free Soil Party had been founded as a single-issue party concerned about the expansion of slavery into new territories. The Compromise of 1850 dealt with that question directly, rendering the party somewhat obsolete. This was augmented by the defection of many Free Soilers back to their party of origin after this time, as well as dismal numbers in the 1852 presidential election. The result was that, by 1854, the Free Soil Party was floundering without a clear way forward.

As we also saw previously, the Kansas-Nebraska Act was such an explosive issue in its day that a minor civil war erupted in the Kansas territory after it was passed. Anti-slavery Whigs (and especially "Conscience Whigs") saw it as the final insult from the southern slave power. Free Soilers saw it as the epitaph on the tombstone of their hopes for a western economy free from the competition of slave labor.

As a result, these disaffected Whigs and Free Soilers (as well as other anti-slavery advocates) began to meet in early 1854 to discuss a way forward in light of what was seen as a major victory for Democrats in general and slavery in particular. By June of that year, less than a month after the Kansas-Nebraska bill was passed on strict party lines, New York journalist Horace Greeley gave the movement its name: "We should not care much whether [we are called] 'Whigs,' 'Free Democrats,' or something else; though we think some simple name like 'Republican' would more fitly designate [us]."

The new Republican coalition of Free Soilers, Conscience Whigs, and previously unaffiliated anti-slavery advocates, held their first nominating convention in 1856 in Philadelphia. There, they nominated former California Senator John C. Fremont for the presidency. Former Illinois Whig leader Abraham Lincoln came in second on the vice-presidential balloting to William L. Dayton of New Jersey.

In the general election that year, Democrat James Buchanan won only 45% of the popular vote, but the Republican ticket was split by a third party run by former Whig president Millard Fillmore, who took more than 20% of the popular vote. Nevertheless, Fremont and the Republicans carried eleven states, showing that this new party, despite its infancy, was poised for future success.

The election also demonstrated, however, that the country had become split down the middle on the issue of slavery: Fremont, representing the anti-slavery Republican Party, won a clear majority of the votes in the northern states, yet received only about 600 *total* votes among the southern states. He did not win a single county south of Kentucky.

The initial platform of the Republican Party was, of course, dominated by opposition to slavery in general, and to the expansion of slavery westward in particular, picking up, as it were, where the Free Soil Party had left off. Their initial platform, however, also called for internal improvements along rivers and harbor areas, a transcontinental railroad (which was also supported by Democrats), and the admittance of the Kansas territory to the Union as a free state – which ultimately took place in 1861.

James Buchanan, now the Democratic president, warned that a Republican victory in 1860 could lead to civil war (he had argued this during the 1856 campaign as well). In 1859, while discussing the recent slave rebellion at Harpers Ferry, West Virginia, he stated that abolitionism "is an incurable disease in the public mind, which may break out in still more dangerous outrages and terminate at last in an open war by the North to abolish slavery in the South." In that same address, he later remarked about the anti-slavery element:

> Those who announce abstract doctrines subversive of the Constitution and the Union must not be surprised should their heated partisans advance one step further and attempt by violence to carry these doctrines into practical effect.

We saw previously that the 1860 presidential campaign created a major split in the Democratic Party. Three different candidates were nominated regionally among southern, northern, and border-state Democrats. This ideological split among Democrats over the question of slavery permitted former-Whig-now-Republican Abraham Lincoln to win the election with only 39% of the popular vote. The southern states, beginning with South Carolina, immediately seceded and within the first few months of Lincoln's term, the Civil War had begun. Among the eleven states that seceded, the only one where Lincoln had received *any votes at all* was Virginia, where he had garnered about 1% of the popular vote. In the ten remaining states, Lincoln had not even been on the ballot.

With the southern states no longer part of the Union, the U.S. government, by default, became dominated by Republicans. In addition to leading the war, they also began instituting policy changes that had been on the "wish list" of National Republicans, Whigs, and Free Soilers for decades. Creating a system of modernization, they first passed the aforementioned Homestead Act, followed by the National Banking Act of 1863, which established federal banks around the nation. Additionally, they created a slew of new taxes to raise money for the war effort, including the first federal income tax (which ended after the war), as well as a high tariff to protect local industries from foreign competition.

Finally, the Republicans of the Lincoln era also began issuing paper money for the first time, called United States Notes. This was a highly controversial move at the time, because many people believed the Constitution forbad the federal government from issuing paper money – in the prevailing view of the time, issuing paper money was a right reserved to the states. People also justifiably feared that paper money would be subject to inflation and value fluctuations, unlike gold and silver which tended to remain stable over long periods of time.

Despite this, Republicans successfully argued that paper money was needed to help pay for the war, and the government had the right to issue the money as part of the war powers granted to Congress.

Though numerous laws would be passed later to regulate this federal paper money, it remained in circulation as the primary currency until the 1970s, when it was replaced by the modern Federal Reserve Note.

The election of Abraham Lincoln ushered in a Golden Age for the Republican Party. They lost only two presidential elections throughout the remainder of the century, both to the same Democrat (Grover Cleveland). There continued, however, to be internal factions squabbling for power.

In 1864, the Republicans became dominated by the so-called Radical Republicans, who viewed Lincoln's attitude toward slavery as too weak. They disliked his appointment of Democrat George McClellan (who had openly condemned the abolitionist movement) as commander of the Union armies, and they criticized Lincoln's Emancipation Proclamation for leaving a significant number of people in servitude (only those slaves held, as of January 1, 1863, in territories still in rebellion were marked for emancipation; slaves in loyal states, or regions already under the control of the Union, remained slaves). They also felt that Lincoln was too conciliatory toward the South, its political and military leaders, and its soldiers. Additionally, they wanted not only a complete abolition of slavery, but they wanted it without compensation to the owners, while Lincoln preferred for the federal government to compensate owners for the loss of their slaves. In 1864, Republicans in Congress passed a Reconstruction bill that included many of these provisions; Lincoln vetoed it.

This ultimately resulted in a strange presidential campaign in 1864. The Radical Republicans broke off from the main Republican Party and nominated the original Republican candidate of 1856, John C. Fremont, for the presidency. They called themselves the Radical Democracy Party.

Greatly weakened by this defection, moderate Republicans joined together with the War Democrats (that faction of northern Democrats who favored Lincoln's policies) and effectively formed a bipartisan coalition that they dubbed the National Union Party. This party held a convention in the summer of 1864 and nominated Lincoln for re-election. They failed, however, to re-nominate his vice-president, Hannibal Hamlin, who had become associated with the Radical Republicans. Instead, they nominated War Democrat Andrew Johnson as Lincoln's running mate, illustrating their aim of bipartisanship.

The result of all this, of course, is that there was *no actual Republican candidate for the presidency in 1864*, and Lincoln served his very brief second term from the National Union coalition, rather than the Republican Party. It also means that when Johnson took over after Lincoln's assassination, his presidency was technically a Democratic presidency, although he continued to use the National Union label in a failed effort to build it into a legitimate political party. He ran for re-election in 1868 as a Democrat, but failed to win the nomination.

The Radical Republican coalition ruled Congress throughout the Reconstruction period of the late 1860's, and had a strong enough majority to override many of the vetoes of Andrew Johnson. They grew to detest Johnson for the same reasons they had abandoned Lincoln – they viewed Johnson as too soft on the Confederacy and too weak on the issue of civil rights for freed slaves. In February of 1868, the Republican-dominated House of Representatives impeached him and voted overwhelmingly to remove him from office for replacing a member of his cabinet without Congressional approval (a law that had been enacted just a year earlier), but the Senate acquitted him by a single vote.

For a brief period in the late 1860s and early 1870s, the Republican Party became so dominant, even within the newly re-admitted southern states (where Republican-backed military governments were still largely in place), that during the 1872 presidential election, the two major tickets consisted of two Republican factions. The first was the mainline Republican faction, which re-nominated sitting president Ulysses S. Grant, and the second was the so-called Liberal Republicans, who nominated long-time abolitionist and civil rights proponent, newspaper editor Horace Greeley.

The Liberal Republicans broke away from the mainline Republican Party for several reasons. To begin with, they felt that Grant's administration had become hopelessly corrupt, a criticism that dogged him throughout his presidency, and which was undoubtedly true. Additionally, they felt that the Reconstruction period was justifiably over and thus disagreed with Grant's decision to keep many of the southern states under military occupation. They argued for a complete reform of the civil service system (the so-called "patronage" or "spoils" system that would later become the target of Democrats and moderate Republicans). And finally, they pushed for total amnesty to ex-Confederates, many of whom (based on an 1866 law) were not permitted to vote or hold office.

By 1872, the Democratic Party had become so disorganized and ineffective on the national level that they chose not to nominate a member of the own party, and instead simply supported the ticket of Horace Greeley. This was viewed as strange by many people at the time, because Greeley had been one of the Democratic Party's most vocal and consistent critics.

In the end, Grant won in a landslide, but the ultimate outcome of this already bizarre election took another bizarre turn when Greeley's wife died right before the election. Greeley and his wife had had a famously unhappy marriage, with five of their seven children dying in childhood and Greeley widely known to be a neglectful husband.

Despite this, Greeley was devastated by his wife's death, which was followed immediately by an enormous loss in the presidential election, and Greeley himself ended up following his wife to the grave before November was out. He became the only presidential candidate to die before the casting of the Electoral College vote (which occurs in early December).

As a result of his death, the 66 electoral votes he secured in the general election were parsed out to other politicians, based on the preferences of the Greeley electors. Three Georgia electors, however, went ahead and cast their votes for Greeley. The result was that six different people won electoral votes in the 1872 election, including one dead man.

In the last quarter of the 19th century, Republicans remained dominant at the national level, although internal disputes and defections led to a series of close elections with Democrats throughout the 1880s and 1890s. As their Whig fathers had before them, Republicans supported industrialization, high tariffs, and the banking industry, while downplaying labor and agricultural interests, but they also became increasingly dominated by, and subsequently fractured by, moralistic issues, particularly prohibition.

Throughout the 19th century, there had been several movements aimed at involving the government in curbing "sin" industries, and this issue eventually became solidified under the Republicans. By the end of the 19th century, the Republican Party was widely viewed as the "dry" party, while the Democrats represented the party of the "wets."

This split between Republicans and Democrats was also seen in the ethnic and religious backgrounds of the various party members. While Democrats tended to appeal to Catholics, Episcopalians, and Lutherans (who were largely anti-prohibition and were mostly of Irish, French, and German heritage), the Republicans became associated with Protestant groups like Methodists, Baptists, and Congregationalists (who had long spear-headed the temperance movement and who were mostly of British, Dutch, and Scandinavian ancestry).

This issue of "sin" industries in general, and prohibition in particular, would reach its catastrophic climax early in the 20th century.

By the Numbers:

The Republican Party of the 19th Century

Founded: circa 1854

Period of Activity: Ongoing

Party Slogans: "Free Soil, Free Labor, Free Speech, Free Men, and Fremont" (1856, adapted from the old Free Soil Party slogan); "Vote As You Shot" (1868); "A Full Dinner Pail" (1896)

Number of Presidents: 7 (Abraham Lincoln, Ulysses S. Grant, Rutherford B. Hayes, James A. Garfield, Chester A. Arthur, Benjamin Harrison, William McKinley)

Leading Party Figures: Abraham Lincoln, Horace Greeley, William McKinley, Schuyler Colfax (Speaker of the House during Reconstruction and vice-president during Grant's first term), James G. Blaine (Speaker of the House, Republican presidential nominee in 1884, Secretary of State under Harrison), John Sherman (U.S. Senator from Ohio, Secretary of the Treasury under Hayes, Secretary of State under McKinley, namesake of the landmark Sherman Anti-Trust Act)

Main Platforms: Abolition, Unionism, protective tariffs, industrialization and urbanization, banking, gold standard, temperance, civil rights, anti-trust laws

THE AMERICAN PARTY

THE AMERICAN Party, known more widely as the "Know-Nothing Party," sprang up in the mid-1850s from the ashes of the Whig Party, around the same time as the Republican Party was forming from those same ashes. It declined almost as rapidly as it emerged, but during its few years of activity, it outpaced the burgeoning Republican Party as the main opposition party to the Democrats.

The Know-Nothing movement had its roots in nativism: an anti-immigration ideology that began to appear in the 1830s. Nativists were Protestant, English-speaking Americans with mostly British ancestry who were concerned with the increasing number of immigrants arriving in America's cities, the majority of whom were Catholic and non-British, frequently did not speak English, and often were suspected of not being "republicans" at heart (that is, adherents to the democratic values of a republican form of government). Catholics of Irish, German, and French ancestry were the primary targets for the nativist movement.

Between 1790 and 1830, there was very little immigration to the United States. The country, at that time, was still a small nation struggling to create an identity for itself on a mostly unsettled continent. In addition, foreign people were fully aware of America's institution of slavery, its laws against naturalization for anyone who was not white, and its continuing problems with hostile Indian tribes. As such, it did not hold great appeal for foreign-born people intent on emigrating.

This view of America began to change after the U.S. victory over Great Britain in the War of 1812, and the virtual economic and political Golden Age that followed it during the presidency of James Monroe (the so-called "Era of Good Feelings"). Foreign-born people, particularly Europeans, began immigrating to the United States in large numbers. U.S. Census records, for instance, show that between 1820 and 1830, more than 140,000 immigrants arrived in the United States (no firm immigration records exist before that time, but historians estimate roughly 60,000 immigrants arrived each decade prior to 1820). From 1830 to 1840, that number jumped to almost 600,000. Between 1840 and 1850, 1.7 million immigrants arrived.

In 1830, immigrants represented roughly 1.6% of the total U.S. population. That number had not changed much since 1790. By 1850, immigrants represented nearly 10% of the U.S. population.

This wave of immigration naturally led to a backlash, and that backlash was represented by the nativist movement, which developed and grew virtually simultaneously with the growth of immigration. Several small nativist political parties sprang up, including the Native American Party, which operated in the mid-1840s, primarily in New York. The name of this party referred not to "Native Americans" as we know them today – that is, American Indians – but to white Protestants whose families had been in America from *before* the Revolutionary War (hence, "native" to the United States).

The Know-Nothings represented the culmination of this nativist movement, and ultimately grew (along with their nickname) out of several secretive, anti-Catholic orders that operated throughout the 1830s and 40s. That tradition of secretiveness was planted into the roots of the American Party, and when a member was asked about the party's doctrines, his reply was said to be: "I know nothing."

The Know-Nothing movement swept into national prominence in 1854 when it took control of the Massachusetts state legislature. Members won offices throughout other states as well – in many cases because their candidates hid their Know-Nothing associations until after the election. In Philadelphia, for instance, a Whig candidate won the mayoral election in a landslide, only revealing later that he was part of the Know-Nothing movement. Know-Nothings also won the mayor's office in Washington, D.C., and San Francisco, and a Know-Nothing was elected governor of California.

The movement also achieved success at the federal level: Know-Nothings won 52 seats in the House of Representatives, and one of those men, Nathanial P. Banks, was elected Speaker of the House (though by the time this happened, Banks had allied with the new Republican Party).

Following these successes, the movement adopted the American Party label and began working on a national level. It very quickly attracted many new members, drawing on the distrust of foreigners so inherent in many Americans of the time.

Its party platform was an exercise in extremism: it wished to limit immigration with legislation that would require a 21-year wait period for an immigrant to gain citizenship; it sought to limit public school teaching positions to white Protestants; it sought to make English the official language of the United States; it promoted a government mandate on daily Bible reading in schools; and it sought to limit elected offices to native-born Americans of Protestant heritage and British or Scottish ancestry.

The party drew support from former Whigs as well as disaffected northern Democrats. Its opposition to the sale of liquor brought it wide-spread support from prohibitionists. It was strongest in the North, where most new immigrants lived (and thus where Americans were most likely to be opposed to immigration), but gained support in the South from slave-holding former Whigs who were sympathetic to the "plight" of northern Americans "overrun" by Catholic immigrants.

During its brief, but meteoric, popularity, the party even attracted voters who were not native-born Americans. According to Harvard historian William E. Gienapp, American Party candidates frequently won as much as 25% of the vote from naturalized German, Dutch, and British voters. They voted for the party not because of its anti-immigration stance, but because of its anti-Catholic stance.

Like most radical political parties, the American Party was frequently embroiled not just in controversy, but even full-blown violence. In the 1855 mayoral election in Louisville, Kentucky, American Party members became convinced that non-citizen Catholic immigrants would attempt to vote. Party members patrolled the polling places throughout the day, and as tensions began to overflow by the evening, riots broke out across the city's Catholic neighborhoods, resulting in the deaths of over twenty Irish and German Catholics, mostly due to fires set by the Know-Nothing mob. The American Party candidate, John Barbee, won the election.

Though the party was growing and gaining rapid popularity, there was also a strong backlash against its extreme views. In a letter to his friend Joshua Speed in 1855, Abraham Lincoln wrote:

> As a nation, we began by declaring that "all men are created equal" ... When the Know-Nothings get control, it will read "all mean are created equal, except negroes, and foreigners, and Catholics." When it comes to this, I should prefer emigrating to some country where they make no pretense of loving liberty – to Russia, for instance, where despotism can be taken pure, and without the base alloy of hypocrisy.

Lincoln preferred Russia, because at least in Russia, people didn't *pretend* to believe in equality and liberty!

The anti-immigration philosophy of the American Party is not difficult to understand: such ideologies have continued to play a prominent role in American politics right up to the present day. Some readers, however, may be perplexed at the strong anti-Catholic sentiment represented by the Know-Nothing movement. The simple explanation is that the Know-Nothings were committed Protestants with deeply-held Protestant convictions; they viewed Catholicism not only as a twisted version of the Christian faith, but also as *inherently anti-republican*. In the mind of the average Know-Nothing, if a group of people were committed to a king-like figure in Rome (the pope), and aristocrat-like figures in the various cardinals and bishops, they couldn't possibly be committed to America's anti-monarchy, republican ideals. And the pope, of course, was not just some random king-like figure in Europe, but the very embodiment of the Anti-Christ to many self-respecting Know-Nothings. Some Know-Nothings, in fact, went so far as to suggest that Catholics might take control of the federal government and make it a pawn of the Roman Catholic Church.

This religious fervor underpinning the movement is undoubtedly what drove its political platforms and ideologies.

In 1856, the American Party ran its first candidate for president. Their prominence in American politics at the time was reflected in their choice: their nomination went to former president Millard Fillmore, who had served in the White House from 1850 to 1853 following the death of Zachary Taylor. A New Yorker, Fillmore not only brought legitimacy to the ticket, but helped secure the northern vote for the party. The vice-presidential nomination went to another prominent figure – Tennessee's Andrew Jackson Donelson, who was the nephew of Andrew Jackson, and was thus designed to draw votes from the Democratic South.

Despite accepting (and even campaigning for) the nomination, however, Fillmore distanced himself from the party's nativist and anti-Catholic stances, focusing more on preserving the Union in the face of the growing problem of slavery. He even had an audience with the pope during a trip to Rome in early 1856. This weakened his position within the party, particularly in the North, but the ticket still managed to win the state of Maryland, and, overall, more than 20% of the popular vote. It would be the best showing by a third party candidate until Theodore Roosevelt's third-party run in 1912.

Following the 1856 election, the party disintegrated very quickly. Despite the strong showing in the presidential election, the question of slavery was beginning to overtake all politics in the country. People were becoming less concerned about immigrants and Catholics, and more concerned about secession and civil war. The American Party's refusal to take a firm stand on the question of slavery made it irrelevant for its slave-holding southern faction, and unacceptable for its anti-slavery northern supporters. It was virtually defunct by 1860.

By the Numbers:

The American Party

Founded: circa 1849 (officially organized in 1854)

Period of Activity: Less than ten years

Party Slogans: "I Know Nothing"

Number of Presidents: 0 (Millard Fillmore was nominated in 1856 and had one of the best third party showings in U.S. history)

Leading Party Figures: J. Neely Johnson (governor of California and later justice of the Nevada Supreme Court), Millard Fillmore, Nathanial P. Banks, Sam Houston (an "outsider" Democrat his whole life, Houston briefly joined the American Party during its height in the mid-1850s, while he was a U.S. Senator from Texas), John J. Crittenden (U.S. Congressman and Senator from Kentucky, Kentucky Governor, 2-time U.S. Attorney General)

Main Platforms: Anti-immigration, anti-Catholicism, prohibition, Unionism

THE OPPOSITION PARTY AND THE CONSTITUTIONAL UNION PARTY

THE OPPOSITION Party was not a true political party, but rather a coalition of factions that united together in opposition of the Democratic Party in the mid-1850s. With the Whig Party fractured and no longer operational on the national level, and only the extremist American Party with any national organization behind it, many former Whigs (particularly anti-slavery Whigs) and other non-Democrats in Congress began voting together under the Opposition Party moniker, making them effectively Independents by our modern standards.

The 34th Congress was elected in 1854 and took office in 1855, and that congressional term remains the only one in U.S. history where there was no majority party, but rather a majority coalition opposed to the minority party (in this case, the Democrats). At least 100 members of Congress counted themselves among the Opposition, while Democrats had only 83 members, and Know-Nothings (the American Party) had about 50.

This, of course, made for a contentious situation in Congress: the Opposition Party had more members than any other party, but not a majority of the total votes. Indeed, *no* party had enough voting power to get any legislation passed. This deadlock was, perhaps, best illustrated by the fact that it took two months for the 34th Congress to choose a Speaker of the House; it was the longest debate in U.S. history for choosing a Speaker. After withdrawing his name from consideration, Ohio congressman Lewis Campbell would note: "The struggle to elect a Speaker has been surrounded with much embarrassment."

As we saw in the previous chapter, the nod finally went to Know-Nothing Nathaniel P. Banks, who, because of his anti-slavery stance, was able to draw enough votes from the Oppositionists to win the seat.

Unfortunately, the problems for the 34th Congress did not end with the election of a Speaker. They failed to pass any major legislation (in the records, the most frequently mentioned legislation from the 34th Congress is a bill governing guano-mining claims on uninhabited islands), and most of the 2-year term was focused on the increasing problem of slavery and its expansion into new territories.

In May of 1856, Democrat Preston Brooks attacked Oppositionist Charles Sumner after Sumner delivered an impassioned speech against the supporters of slavery. The attack occurred right on the floor of the Senate chamber, and Brooks wielded a cane to beat Sumner to the floor. He suffered severe head trauma, a spinal cord injury, and what is recognized today as Post-Traumatic Stress Disorder. It would be three years before he was able to return to full-time duties in the Senate. Pro-slavery Democrats ridiculed him for this long convalescence, suggesting it proved he was a weakling and a coward.

As the Republican Party began to grow, most Oppositionists (former Whigs, Free Soilers, and others) joined this new party. However, a number of Oppositionists did not share the strong anti-slavery position of the Republicans, and instead joined a new coalition going by the title of the Constitutional Union Party. The goal of this party was to side-step the question of slavery all together and find a way to preserve the Union in the face of the growing threat of secession.

The Constitutional Union Party was primarily made up of these former Whigs-turned-Oppositionists, as well as former Know-Nothings and a few Southern Democrats who were more concerned about disunion than slavery. Their platform was short: a mere two paragraphs stating, in part: "…it is both the part of patriotism and of duty to recognize no political principle other than the Constitution of the Country, the Union of the States, and the Enforcement of the Laws."

John J. Crittenden, a U.S. Senator from Kentucky, protégé of Henry Clay, and a former Whig-turned-Know-Nothing, led the creation of the new party in late 1859 and early 1860. His mentor, Clay, had been famous for finding ways to compromise great political disputes, earning him the nickname "The Great

Compromiser," and Crittenden saw himself as following in the great Clay's footsteps. In December of 1860, when the secession crisis finally became a reality, he authored a series of resolutions and bills known collectively as the Crittenden Compromise, which aimed to avert war and bring the country back together. Congress, however, failed to pass it.

The new party held a nominating convention in May of 1860, with John J. Crittenden as the obvious choice. Crittenden, however, was already over 70 years of age by this time, and declined to be considered. Instead, the nomination became a battle between Sam Houston of Texas and John Bell of Tennessee. Bell was a southerner and a slave-owner, but he had been an early supporter of the Whig Party in the 1830s, opposed to the politics of Andrew Jackson, and had opposed the expansion of slavery in the 1850s, voting against the Kansas-Nebraska Act – the only southern congressman to do so. This made him a perfect candidate for the new party, whose goal was to sidestep the question of slavery and create compromise.

Their vice-presidential candidate also fit well with the party's desire to avoid the question of slavery: they nominated former Secretary of State under Millard Fillmore, and Massachusetts Senator, Edward Everett, who had been forced by public pressure to resign his Senate seat a few weeks after the Kansas-Nebraska Act had been passed, because he had refused to vote on the bill. He considered himself anti-slavery, but did not want to polarize southerners by voting against the bill. He also, however, recognized the political damage he might sustain in Massachusetts if he voted in favor of it. Instead, he didn't vote. Public outcry over his refusal to take a stance forced him to resign anyway.

The Constitutional Union Party ticket managed to win three states in the 1860 election – Kentucky, Tennessee, and Virginia – good enough to finish ahead of Northern Democrat Stephen Douglas in electoral votes, but it came in a distant forth in the popular vote, winning only 12%.

The country was clearly finished compromising on slavery, and the Constitutional Union Party's unwillingness to take a firm stance one way or the other was ultimately its undoing. It disappeared after the 1860 election.

By the Numbers:

The Constitutional Union Party

Founded: 1860 (origins in the Opposition Party of 1854-1858)

Period of Activity: One year

Party Slogans: "The Union As It Is;" "Liberty and Union"

Number of Presidents: 0 (John Bell won three states in the 1860 presidential election, but only by a plurality)

Leading Party Figures: John J. Crittenden, Sam Houston, John Bell, Edward Everett

Main Platforms: Constitutionalism, Unionism

THE PEOPLE'S PARTY

IN THE DECADES following the Civil War, the United States began growing rapidly into a wealthy, modern, industrialized world power. It continued to widen its territory with new western states, and saw a dramatic increase in population, both through new births and several waves of immigration. For instance, in the seventy years between 1790 and 1860, the U.S. added roughly 26 million people. For the forty years following that – from 1860 to 1900 – over 45 million were added. This included roughly nine million immigrants between 1880 and 1900.

One of the results of this social, cultural, and political change was the entrenchment of the Democratic Party and the Republican Party as the two primary political parties in the United States. As we have seen in the preceding chapters, most of American history up to this time had been characterized by a 2-party system – one party in power, and the other in opposition – but the parties themselves had not always been the same. Parties had come and gone, risen into prominence for a few years or decades, then fallen by the wayside to be replaced by another party.

The events of the latter part of the 19th century changed that variable aspect of partisan politics and led to the situation still in place in the 21st century – Democrats on one side, Republicans on the other, and every other group a perpetual third party with little hope of ever breaking the control of the two dominate powers.

In the late 19th century, as Democrats and Republicans became the two elite parties in America's political system, a backlash against *both* parties began in rural areas of the country, leading to the formation of the so-called Populist Movement.

Populism is a political ideology that seeks to establish the rights of "the people" over the rights of the powerful elite. In the case of the Populist Movement of the 19th century, "the people" were the farmers and laborers of America's heartland, and the "powerful elite" were the urban capitalists and industrialists who were seen by "the people" as controlling both the Republican *and* Democratic parties, to the detriment of the common man.

The result was the People's Party, which was officially formed in 1892 from a coalition of small farmers and labor groups.

Meeting in Omaha, Nebraska, in a nominating convention for the 1892 presidential election, the People's Party adopted what has come to be known as the Omaha Platform. Written by a former Minnesota congressman named Ignatius Donnelly, the preamble states the basic ideology of the movement: "The fruits of the toil of millions are boldly stolen to build up colossal fortunes for a few ... From the same prolific womb of governmental injustice we breed the two great classes – tramps and millionaires." The preamble goes on to make clear just who is responsible for this situation: "We have witnessed for more than a quarter of a century the struggles of the two great political parties for power and plunder, while grievous wrongs have been inflicted upon the suffering people."

Among other things, the platform echoed Andrew Jackson's long-ago struggle against the Second Bank of the United States, calling for the dissolution of the national banking system, which had been established during the Lincoln administration in the early 1860s, and which the Populists viewed as a corrupt, tyrannical tool of the elite.

Additionally, the platform called for a slew of other reforms, many of which would be enacted in decades to come:

1. An 8-hour work day.
2. A graduated income tax to help relieve the tax burden carried by businesses.
3. Direct election of U.S. Senators by popular vote.
4. A one-year term limit for presidents.
5. Government ownership of all railroads, telephones, and telegraphs.
6. Elimination of all federal subsidies for private businesses.
7. Establishment of silver as a legal currency.
8. New immigration restrictions to help reduce the "pauper and criminal classes" and open more jobs for Americans.

9. Complete abolition of the Pinkerton National Detective Agency.

Why would a political party be concerned with the break-up of a detective agency? Allen Pinkerton, a lawyer-turned-security specialist, had become famous in the 1860s after he foiled a plot to assassinate Abraham Lincoln prior to his inauguration. His detective and security organization grew so large in the ensuing decades that by the 1890s, he had more than 30,000 personnel around the country, making his organization larger than the United States Army. Furthermore, in the 1870s, Congress had instructed the newly-formed Department of Justice to create a unit charged with investigating and prosecuting federal crimes. The Bureau of Investigation (later known as the FBI) would be formed for this purpose in 1908, but in the 1870s, the Department of Justice didn't have enough resources to create such a unit. Instead, they contracted the work to the Pinkerton agency – effectively making the Pinkerton agency a federal police force.

With the legitimacy of the federal government behind it, the Pinkerton agency grew increasingly powerful, and wealthy businessmen would frequently hire Pinkerton agents to infiltrate unions and break up labor strikes.

For this reason, the People's Party, with its pro-labor, anti-elitist ideology, viewed Pinkerton as little more than a federally-subsidized goon squad. In the words of the official party platform: "We regard the maintenance of a large standing army of mercenaries [the Pinkerton agency] as a menace to our liberties."

They were perhaps closer to the mark than one might suspect. A little over a month after the party platform was adopted, Pinkerton agents were hired to break a strike at the Homestead Steel Works in Pennsylvania. A gunfight broke out between the two sides, with both sides claiming the other fired first. The result was fifteen deaths and several dozen injuries.

The People's Party did not succeed in having the Pinkerton agency shut down (in fact, it existed until 2003), but in 1893, Congress passed a law limiting the government's ability to hire strikebreakers, and specifically barred Pinkerton detectives from working for the federal government. It became known as the Anti-Pinkerton Act, and it is still in force today.

In addition to adopting the Omaha Platform at their 1892 convention, the People's Party also nominated former U.S. congressman James B. Weaver for the presidency. A former Republican, Weaver had been elected to Congress in 1878 as a member of the Greenback Party, a single-issue party that advocated bimetallism – that is, they opposed the Gold Standard, wanted silver made into legal tender along with gold, and wanted the government to issue paper currency, as it had done during the Civil War (hence the name "Greenback"). Weaver was up for re-election in 1880 for the same party, but was instead nominated for president on the Greenback ticket that year. He went on to win about 3% of the popular vote.

By 1892, the Greenback Party was defunct and many of its members had become part of the Populist Movement.

Weaver and the People's Party failed to win in the general election, but had one of the best third party showings in U.S. history, winning roughly 9% of the popular vote and carrying the electoral votes of four states. Three of the four states won by Weaver had been carried by incumbent Republican Benjamin Harrison four years earlier, and it is likely that Weaver's candidacy helped ensure Harrison's failure to win re-election. Democrat Grover Cleveland, who had served as president from 1884 to 1888, defeated Harrison by 400,000 votes; Weaver had won more than one million votes, the majority of which would likely have gone to Harrison, as both Republicans and Populists opposed the Democrat's Gold Standard, the leading issue in the race. Many Populists (such as Weaver), had originally been defectors from the Republican Party in the 1870s and 80s.

The People's Party faded into oblivion after the mid-1890s, but, as we have seen, many of their platforms and ideologies were eventually adopted by other parties and enacted by subsequent congresses and administrations. The Democrats, long-time defenders of the Gold Standard, began to promote bimetallism in the late 1890s, although they ultimately lost the battle. However, the

8-hour workday was eventually adopted, as well as an income tax and the direct election of U.S. Senators by popular vote.

The People's Party was one of the first significant parties in American history to widely promote women's rights. Frances Willard, head of the Christian Women's Temperance Union and a highly influential voice in the women's suffrage movement, chaired the People's Party convention in 1892, though she herself could not vote in the general election.

In 1896, instead of nominating their own candidate for the presidency, the weakening People's Party supported the candidacy of Democrat William Jennings Bryan, a fierce opponent of the Gold Standard. Jennings lost to Republican William McKinley. The party nominated banker, publisher, and former Republican Wharton Barker for the presidency in 1900, with Ignatius Donnelly – who had penned the preamble to the Omaha Platform – as his running mate. They won only 50,000 votes – less than 0.5% of the popular vote.

Though it failed to win any presidential elections, the People's Party had significant success throughout the 1890s at the state level, seating eleven governors in nine different states and almost fifty U.S. congressmen from among the South and West.

By the Numbers:

The People's Party

Founded: 1891 (origins in the Populist Movement and the Greenback Party of the 1870s and 80s)

Period of Activity: About ten years

Party Slogans: "Equal Rights to All; Special Privileges to None"

Number of Presidents: 0 (in 1892, James B. Weaver had the best third party showing of any candidate between 1860 and 1912, winning four states in the general election)

Leading Party Figures: James B. Weaver, Ignatius Donnelly, Wharton Barker, Marion Butler (U.S. Senator from North Carolina)

Main Platforms: Anti-elitism, bimetallism, agrarianism, labor unions, wealth distribution

POLITICAL PARTIES OF THE 20TH and 21st CENTURIES

THE SOCIALIST PARTY OF AMERICA

IN THE LATE 19th century, several different minor political parties with Marxist tendencies had started forming, most notably the Socialist Labor Party, which began operating in the 1870s, and the Social Democratic Party, which formed in the late 1890s and secured nearly 90,000 votes in the 1900 presidential election.

By the turn of the century, the Socialist Labor Party split due to internal disagreements over the direction of its leader. In 1901, those who had left the party came together with the newer and more moderate Social Democratic Party to form a coalition which they dubbed the Socialist Party of America.

Socialism is an ideology that sprang from the economic writings of 19th century German philosophers Karl Marx and Friedrich Engels. Socialism and Marxism are not necessarily the same thing: Socialism is simply a national economic structure formulated from the ideas and ideals expressed by Marxist philosophy. To fully understand the goal of Socialism, it is necessary first to understand the capitalist system that Socialism has sought to overturn. Keep in mind that both Socialism and Capitalism are *economic* systems, not political systems. It is perfectly possible to have a democratic government with a socialist economic system, or an authoritarian government with a capitalist system. Most governments, including the modern United States, combine the two economic systems to a greater or lesser degree.

In a capitalist society, such as the United States, businesses that make and sell products are owned by private individuals and shareholders. Except in the cases of very small businesses, these owners and shareholders don't actually produce the goods they sell. Instead, the production is done by employees who work for the owners. For instance, the shareholders of a car company are not actually working on the production line assembling automobiles;

they have simply invested money in the company and therefore earn profits when the company does well.

Because of the great wealth often collected by corporate owners and shareholders, they are able to gain political power and influence and thus ensure their own interests are protected in the political arena.

One of the side-effects of any capitalist system is the formation and continuation of social classes, with the wealthy representing a small percentage, with a lot of power, at the top of the food chain, the middle class representing a very large percentage, with limited power, in the middle of the food chain, and the poorer classes struggling at the bottom with virtually no power. It is impossible to eliminate poverty in a capitalist system because the very system itself is built on the notion that some people will win and some will lose.

Based on Marxist thought, the socialist system sought (and continues to seek) to remedy that problem of social stratification by creating an economic and political system that would put the power of production in the hands of the laborers – the people who actually produce the products that are bought and sold. Instead of being owned by private shareholders, a company in the socialist model would be owned collectively by the people who work for the company – there would be no shareholders or private owners. In the car company analogy from above, the assembly line employees, themselves, would be the owners of the company. As a result, the employees of the company would be the primary beneficiaries of the company's profits, rather than private investors who don't actually work for the company. This dichotomy – between the laborers who actually make the product, and the owners who simply invest money in the company's success – is a major focal point of socialist ideology. In the socialist worldview, the shareholders exploit the laborers.

In an ideal socialist society, the government would control production (those companies that produce goods needed by all people, such as food, shelter, water, clothes, oil, transportation, telecommunications, energy, etc.). The government would be funded not through taxes (as in a capitalist system), but through the profits of the state-owned manufacturing companies. These profits would, in turn, be used to grow the businesses and provide wealth distribution to support the people. Other companies – those *selling* the goods made by the state-owned companies, as well as companies making products which weren't necessarily needed by everyone (this would include *most* businesses) – would ideally be collectively owned by their employees, rather than private owners/investors.

The ultimate goal of this socialist model is a classless society where everyone does their part, everyone reaps equally large benefits from their labor, and everyone is well-fed, well-cared-for, and able to pursue their own interests and aspirations. When a society has reached this sort of socialist ideal, it is termed a "communist" society – a communal society where everyone works together for the greater good. When the communist ideal is finally reached, "government," in the traditional sense of the word, ceases to exist.

Most social scientists would argue that Socialism and Communism are ultimately two different things, with Socialism being primarily an *economic philosophy* within a traditional political structure, and Communism being primarily a *political philosophy* encompassing socialist ideologies and functioning within a totally different kind of political structure.

The Socialist Party had a great deal of local success in many regions of the country in the first few decades of the 20th century. By the early 1920s, the party had won more than 1,000 elections, including state and U.S. representative offices, and seating almost 100 mayors. The party platform in 1912 called for such things as universal voting rights for women, the abolition of the Electoral College, representation in Congress for the District of Columbia, and healthcare reform (including the formation of an "independent" Bureau of Health). It also called for a shorter workday, no more than a five and a half-day work week, a ban on child labor (under 16 years old), a minimum wage, and the establishment of a pension system for workers. Finally, it called for "collective ownership" of "all large-scale industries," as well as all transportation and communications industries.

Eugene V. Debs, who had run for president in every election since 1900, was the Socialist nominee, and he won nearly a million votes in the election: roughly 6% of the popular vote. This was despite the fact that many conservative party members abandoned the more liberal Debs and voted for the Democratic nominee, Woodrow Wilson.

Following the outbreak of World War One, the party began to splinter over whether to support the war or oppose it. The moderate party leadership largely supported America's involvement in the war, but the more radical, left wing element was vehemently opposed to it. Eugene V. Debs, for instance, gave a speech in 1918 calling for Socialists to evade the draft; he was subsequently arrested, convicted of sedition, and sentenced to ten years in prison. He was pardoned in 1921 by Republican Warren G. Harding.

After the Bolshevik Revolution in 1917, the left wing of the party became more and more radicalized, and by 1919, they were effectively suspended from party operations by the more moderate party leaders. These suspended radicals eventually formed two different Communist parties, which combined in 1929 to form the Communist Party USA, which is still in existence with roughly 2,000 members. At its height, however, the party claimed as many as 60,000 members.

The Socialist Party was greatly weakened by the defection of the radicals and the extremely bad publicity brought by the turmoil (which included the expulsion of five Socialists from the New York State Assembly and a major nationwide crackdown by the Department of Justice on suspected anarchists and revolutionaries within the Socialist Party). By 1921, the party, which had once had more than 100,000 members, had fewer than 15,000.

Throughout the 1920s, the Socialist Party remained largely behind the scenes, though they strongly supported the presidential run of Robert M. La Follette, who ran as a Progressive in 1924 and won nearly 17% of the popular vote.

Following America's entry into the Great Depression, however, the Socialist Party began to regain its footing and strengthen its organization, and by 1932, it had nearly doubled its membership from its pre-Depression level (though it was still well below the numbers seen in the 1910s). Unfortunately, this resurgence brought more factionalism with it, as the party began to grow more radical. The so-called "Old Guard" of the party, which represented moderate, social democratic views, split off and formed the Social Democratic Federation, which largely supported the Democratic presidency of Franklin Roosevelt. It eventually reunited with the Socialist Party, but not until the late 1950s.

Freed of many of the moderate voices of the party, the new leadership in the 1930s led the party to more radical, left wing stances, and controversially opened membership to disaffected Communists. The party adopted a vehement anti-war stance, but encouraged armed rebellion against any possible fascist takeover of the U.S. government. They remained opposed to the Stalin regime in Russia, which they saw as a military dictatorship that distorted the true principles of Marxism.

Factionalism continued to dog the Socialist Party for the remainder of its existence. It ran its last presidential candidate, Pennsylvania politician Darlington Hoopes, in 1956. In the early 1970s, the party reorganized to focus solely on influencing policy debates in the United States. As such, the word "party" was dropped from the name, and the organization became the Social Democrats, USA. Another group formed a new political party called the Socialist Party, USA, which is still in operation.

By the Numbers:

The Socialist Party of America

Founded: 1901

Period of Activity: About seventy years

Party Slogans: "From Each According to His Ability, To Each According to His Need;" "Unite at the Ballot Box" (1912); "Workers of the World Unite"

Number of Presidents: 0 (Eugene V. Debs won nearly a million votes in both 1912 and 1920, despite being in prison for sedition during the 1920 election)

Leading Party Figures: Eugene V. Debs, Allen Benson (Socialist newspaper editor and 1916 presidential candidate), Norman Thomas (6-time presidential candidate), Morris Hillquit (co-founder and party chairman), William D. Haywood (labor union activist and party leader)

Main Platforms: Social democracy, labor unions, women's suffrage, wealth distribution, Marxism, opposition to capitalism and fascism

THE PROGRESSIVE PARTY

THE PROGRESSIVE Party, also called the Bull Moose Party, was founded by Teddy Roosevelt in 1912 as a vehicle for his attempt at winning another term in the White House, following a 4-year retirement from public office. Roosevelt had become president in 1901 upon the death of William McKinley, and had voluntarily retired in 1908, choosing instead to support the candidacy of his Secretary of War and friend, William Howard Taft.

During Taft's time in office, a major political rift grew between the two friends, as Taft's conservative policies deviated from Roosevelt's more progressive ideology. The split between the two former colleagues was mirrored in the Republican Party as a whole, as conservatives and progressives began to become increasingly factionalized over issues like tariffs, conservation, and big business.

By the time the 1912 presidential election rolled around, Roosevelt – who, despite being "retired" from the presidency for four years, was still only 53 – decided to seek the Republican nomination and unseat Taft.

Prior to 1912, presidential candidates were freely chosen by party delegates. These delegates – made up of party loyalists from each state – would come together in a national convention, nominate candidates, debate, argue, and make deals, and finally choose a nominee to be the party's official candidate for president. Over time, however, these conventions came to be heavily influenced by so-called party bosses. Party bosses were powerful regional party leaders who carried a lot of influence over their region's party members, and thus had an undue amount of influence over the nominating convention.

In the eyes of critics, it was the party bosses, working behind the scenes and wielding influence over the delegates, who ultimately chose the party's candidate. These critics viewed the entire process as corrupt, unfair, and undemocratic.

The answer to the problem was the state presidential primary. Voters in each state would go to the polls and choose among the party's candidates. Later, at the national convention, the state's delegates would be required to support whichever candidate the voters chose. This way, the *people* were choosing the candidates, and the party bosses could no longer use their power and influence to threaten, bribe, and coerce delegates into voting for their man.

States began establishing presidential primaries in 1910, and by 1912, twelve states were ready to use the primary system in that year's presidential election.

Roosevelt proved popular among the people. In the twelve states that held primaries, Roosevelt won nine of them, most by landslides. He even won Taft's home state of Ohio. Another candidate, Robert M. La Follette, won two others. Taft won only Massachusetts.

When the Republican National Convention came around, however, Taft's position as the incumbent president, as well as the head of the Republican National Committee, gave him an enormous amount of leverage with the delegations from the remaining 36 states, whose delegates had been chosen in the older fashion through state conventions. Many of these other delegations, however, were contested as a result of party splits at the state level. The Committee – headed by Taft – ultimately had the authority to mediate these contested delegations and assign them to one candidate or the other.

Not surprisingly, the Committee appointed almost all of the contested delegates to Taft – more than 230 votes. It was enough to give Taft the victory – and thus the Republican nomination. Roosevelt, outraged at what he viewed as an egregious abuse of power by Taft and his supporters, encouraged his delegates to abstain from voting and walked out of the convention.

Intent on continuing his candidacy, and convinced he could beat both Taft *and* the Democratic candidate, Woodrow Wilson, Roosevelt and his supporters left the Republican Party and very quickly formed a third party, which they dubbed the Progressive Party. They convened in August of 1912 and adopted a platform that called for a "new party" that would "sweep away the old abuses" of the Republican and Democratic parties. These old parties, the platform argued, were "tools of corrupt interests" that had been used to create a sinister "invisible government" and an "unholy alliance between corrupt business and corrupt politics."

The Progressive platform called for a number of reforms:

1. Direct election of U.S. Senators by popular vote.
2. Establishment of "direct democracy," specifically the referendum and recall vote, including judicial recall (which would allow voters to overrule a court after it finds a law unconstitutional).
3. Women's suffrage.
4. Campaign finance reform.
5. An 8-hour work day and a minimum wage law for female workers.
6. Prohibition of child labor and the establishment of standards for occupational safety and injured worker's compensation.
7. Establishment of social welfare programs for the unemployed, sick, and elderly.
8. A downward revision of the protective tariff, establishment of an inheritance tax, and a law enacting a federal income tax.
9. Establishment of a Department of Labor and a National Health Service.

The Progressive Party was the first prominent political party to support national women's suffrage and to appoint women as party leaders. Jane Addams, a widely-known social worker and suffragist, was invited to speak at the convention, the first time a woman had been given such an honor. A number of women also served as Progressive electors in the Electoral College, and as such became the first women to cast electoral votes in a presidential election.

Late in the campaign season, Teddy Roosevelt was shot by an assassin just before going onstage for a speech in Milwaukee. The bullet struck him in the chest after hitting his rolled up speech and his eyeglass case. Undeterred, Roosevelt went on with the speech, taking the podium and telling the audience: "I don't know whether you fully understand that I have just been shot; but it takes more than that to kill a bull moose."

The party split between Roosevelt and Taft ultimately led to a resounding victory for Woodrow Wilson, who became only the second Democrat to win the White House since before the Civil War. Perhaps most remarkable of all, Roosevelt won more votes than Taft, the only time since the advent of the 2-party system that a major party candidate has been outpolled by a third-party candidate. Taft, in fact, won only two states and carried less than 25% of the popular vote, easily the worst showing by an incumbent president in U.S. history.

In addition to the strong showing in the presidential election, the Progressives also won a number of local elections among the states, and also seated nine members in the U.S. House of Representatives.

In the years following Roosevelt's loss to Wilson, the Progressive Party quickly disintegrated. A few more offices were won by Progressives in 1914 and 1916, but the party never regained its 1912 prominence.

At the national convention in 1916, the party again nominated Roosevelt for president, but he declined the offer, choosing instead to reconcile with the Republican Party. Most of his supporters followed him, and the Progressive Party became virtually defunct by 1918.

In 1924, Robert M. La Follette, one of the founders of the Progressive movement, revived the Progressive Party name and ran for president on a populist platform supporting labor unions and collective bargaining, a strong centralized government, increased taxes on the wealthy, and government ownership of railroads and utilities. His party was also fiercely anti-war, supporting the institution of a referendum vote before any large scale military action.

As the only candidate from any party supporting traditional liberal causes in the 1924 election, La Follette won over 16% of the popular vote, but won only his home state of Wisconsin in the Electoral College.

By the Numbers:

The Progressive Party

Founded: 1912

Period of Activity: About six years (revived for the 1924 presidential election only)

Party Slogans: "A Square Deal All Around"

Number of Presidents: 0 (Teddy Roosevelt had the best showing of any third-party candidate in history in the 1912 presidential election, winning six states)

Leading Party Figures: Teddy Roosevelt, Robert M. La Follette, Hiram Johnson (governor of California, party chairman, and Roosevelt's running mate), Jane Addams (social and political activist)

Main Platforms: Regulation of business, lower tariffs, women's suffrage, workers' rights and protections, social welfare, direct democracy

THE 20ᵀᴴ and 21ˢᵗ CENTURY REPUBLICAN PARTY

THE FIRST three decades of the 20th century saw continued domination, at the national level at least, by the Republican Party. Only one Democrat served in the White House between 1897 and 1933. And, as we saw in the previous chapter, that one Democrat likely only won the White House because of a split in the Republican Party. Following that party meltdown in 1912, the Republicans quickly reunited in 1920 and continued the dominance they had enjoyed since the Civil War.

It was during this era at the beginning of the 20th century that the Republican Party began to cement its alliance with the business and corporate world, thanks in large part to William McKinley and his campaign manager, Mark Hanna, who was also a U.S. Senator from Ohio and a successful businessman. Though both men were dead by 1904, their influence would forever alter the party's relationship with business interests. Promoting high tariffs, the gold standard, railroads, and industry, the Republican Party at the turn of the century created a partnership with corporate America which endures to the present day.

Despite the internal struggles between progressives and conservatives, the party led the nation through an economic boom at the start of the 20th century never before seen in the United States. In 1900, after four years under McKinley, the nation's GDP hit an all-time high of 422 million dollars. It had taken exactly 110 years for the country to reach such a lofty economic number. It took only another 25 years to make that much again, with the GDP reaching 846 million by 1925. It reached 977 million before the stock market crash of 1929 led the nation into the Great Depression.

In addition to promoting economic growth through policies aimed at aiding business and industry, the Republican Party at the start of the 20th century also found itself at the helm of the Prohibition Movement, a moral, religious, and political ideology that had been brewing in American culture since before the Civil War. While both parties had "wet" and "dry" factions, the Republicans became more prominently associated with the movement as temperance supporters gained leadership roles within the party hierarchy. By the second decade of the 20th century, Republican legislators grew increasingly influenced by the powerful lobbying of the Anti-Saloon League, which had been founded in the 1890s and was spearheading the push for a constitutional amendment on the issue.

Furthermore, the same Methodists, Baptists, and Presbyterian groups who had long helped spearhead the temperance movement also largely supported the Republican Party and its officeholders (except in the South, where these same groups instead brought Southern Democrats into the temperance fold).

In late 1917, the 18th Amendment, outlawing the manufacture and distribution of alcohol, was passed by both houses of Congress with strong bipartisan support. By late 1918, enough states had ratified the amendment to put the law into force. Prohibition officially began in January, 1920.

Later that year, Republican Warren G. Harding was elected to the presidency and for the next ten years, Republicans held not only the White House, but also both chambers of Congress. When Harding died in office in 1923, he was replaced by his vice-president, Calvin Coolidge, who was then re-elected in 1924.

By this time, the cracks were beginning to show in the façade of Prohibition, as organized crime began to proliferate around the illegal manufacture of alcohol. Resentment was also beginning to build among Americans who felt that the 18th Amendment and its accompanying enforcement law, the Volstead Act, unfairly impacted the middle and lower classes. Neither the amendment nor the enforcing federal law actually outlawed the possession or consumption of alcohol – only the manufacture, distribution, and sale of it. As a result, wealthier people (including many of the very politicians who were passing dry laws) were able to stockpile wine, liquor, and spirits before Prohibition went into effect, allowing them to continue imbibing as they always had. Alcohol continued to be served and consumed at the White House throughout the entirety of the Prohibition era, and numerous businesses had private stocks available for their executives and stockholders. Over time, this fueled an increasing amount of resentment among everyday people who were not privy to the same luxuries.

The Democrats used this increasing resentment, and especially the growing problem with bootlegging and its offspring of organized crime, to steadily erode the public image of the Republican Party, which held the reins of power. The 1924 Republican Party platform carefully skirted the issue, but the Democratic platform accused the Republicans in power of not properly enforcing the very law they helped create and were in charge of executing. The 1928 Democratic platform made this accusation even more forcefully, and the Democratic candidate for president that year, New York governor Al Smith, was opposed to Prohibition and openly favored repealing the law.

Realizing they needed to make a firm statement about the issue, the Republican platform that year briefly affirmed the party's commitment to upholding the Constitution and the 18th Amendment. Despite continuing concerns about the Republican administration's handling of the law, the Republican candidate, Herbert Hoover, had no trouble keeping the White House in Republican hands, defeating Smith in a landslide.

The 1928 election, however, did serve to draw firmer lines between the two major parties on the issue of Prohibition. The Democrats were now seen more widely as the party of the "wets," while the Republicans, whether intentionally or not, had maneuvered themselves into becoming the party of Prohibition.

United States prosperity, and the future of the Republican Party, all came crashing down in October of 1929, just a few months after Hoover took office, when the bottom dropped out of the stock market. Over the remainder of Hoover's presidency, it continued a steady decline, bottoming out at its lowest level of the entire 20th century in July of 1932. At that point, it had lost 89% of its value. It would be twenty-five years before it returned to its pre-crash peak.

The stock market crash and subsequent Great Depression decimated the Republican Party. As the party in power in both the

White House and Congress for the preceding twelve years, Americans tended to blame the Republicans for the calamity, and especially Herbert Hoover, who had the misfortune to be in office when it all fell apart.

Despite his name being virtually synonymous with the Great Depression, Hoover neither caused the catastrophe nor sat idly by while it grew progressively worse (as is sometimes asserted). In fact, Hoover had spent much of his life as an activist and philanthropist, and though he believed in the basic Republican ideal of limited government, he did take steps to alleviate suffering and get people back to work (for instance, he instituted a number of public works programs that would later become the centerpiece of Roosevelt's New Deal legislation). But his attempts did not go nearly far enough, and many proved hopelessly naïve (such as his attempt to slow the unemployment rate by encouraging businesses to "voluntarily" refuse to lay off workers or cut wages). A fiscal conservative, he also remained committed to keeping a balanced budget, refusing to increase the national debt with welfare spending. Finally, several policies aimed at relieving the depression only made matters worse, including a number of enormous tax increases and, most notably, the Smoot-Hawley Tariff Act. This bill, authored by two Republicans and signed into law in 1930 by Hoover, raised tariffs on imported goods in an effort to encourage Americans to buy American-made products and thus boost the economy. However, numerous other countries, also suffering from depressed economies, retaliated by raising their own tariffs on American goods. The result was that American exports dropped dramatically, ultimately harming the economy even further.

Hoover's strong support for Prohibition only further damaged his credibility in the eyes of the American public. Calls for repeal of the 18th Amendment had been gaining traction throughout the course of Hoover's term, as proponents saw the manufacture and sale of alcohol as a viable way to get a lot of people back to work and spending money.

In the presidential election of 1932, Hoover was defeated in a landslide by Franklin D. Roosevelt, who, vowing to get the economy back on track and repeal the 18th Amendment, won more of the popular vote than any Democrat before him. It was in this election that urban areas, so heavily affected by the Depression, became Democratic strongholds for the first time.

Virtually overnight, the Republican Party's 70-year domination of Washington politics was over. It would be twenty years before another Republican won the White House and fifteen years before Republicans had a majority in either chamber of Congress.

The Great Depression served to factionalize and, in many ways, moderate the Republican Party. As we have seen, the Republicans had a tradition of progressive politics, most notably seen in the presidency of Theodore Roosevelt, but following the disastrous 1912 presidential election, the party had moved to the right. The Great Depression brought moderates back to the forefront of the party again. Moderates like Fiorello La Guardia, Thomas Dewey, and Alf Landon in the 1930s paved the way for later moderates like Nelson Rockefeller, George Romney, and Richard Nixon.

Landon, who generally supported Roosevelt's New Deal, and who had been part of the Progressive Party of Theodore Roosevelt, was the Republican nominee in the 1936 presidential election. Despite his centrism, he lost what was, at the time, the most lopsided presidential election in U.S. history, gaining only 36% of the popular vote and just two states in the Electoral College.

Throughout the 1940s, Republicans continued to run moderate candidates against Roosevelt and later Truman, but none ever came close to winning (Thomas Dewey's 46% in 1944 was the best showing of any Republican between 1932 and 1952).

Despite being controlled at the national level by moderates and centrists, conservatives still dominated among Republicans in Congress. Led by Senator Robert Taft of Ohio (son of William Howard Taft, who had led the conservative wing against Theodore Roosevelt), the conservative Republicans in Congress formed a coalition with conservative Southern Democrats to fight against the legislative agenda of first Roosevelt, and later Truman. This coalition succeeded in the 1940s in repealing several of Roosevelt's New Deal laws. They lost clout on the national scene, however, for their isolationist perspectives regarding the war in Europe, particularly after the Japanese attack on Pearl Harbor.

Throughout the next three decades, the Republican Party continued to be split between conservative and liberal factions. The liberals and moderates dominated in the heavily populated Northeast, while conservatives proliferated in the Midwest and South. The moderates of this era, frequently referred to as "Rockefeller Republicans" (named after New York governor, and later vice-president, Nelson Rockefeller) generally supported the liberal social programs of Roosevelt and later Lyndon Johnson, including the Civil Rights movement, but they remained loyal to the interests of corporate America and continued to believe in balanced budgets. They promoted high taxes to achieve this, and encouraged new business development as a means of growing the economy. It was in this way that they differed dramatically from the conservative faction, which had long believed that tax cuts and reductions in federal spending were a better way to spur economic growth.

Dwight D. Eisenhower, a moderate, became the first Republican president in two decades in 1952, serving two terms under a Congress still controlled by Democrats. Another moderate, Richard Nixon, served as vice-president to Eisenhower, then lost a close election to John F. Kennedy in 1960. Nixon sat out the election of 1964, in which conservative Barry Goldwater lost in an enormous landslide to Lyndon B. Johnson, but Nixon ran again in 1968 and narrowly defeated Democrat Hubert Humphrey. Goldwater was the only conservative Republican to win the Republican nomination for the presidency between 1936 and 1980.

Despite moderates like Nixon and Gerald Ford carrying the party's reigns throughout the 1960s and 70s, the conservative movement gained steam as an inevitable backlash began to brew against high federal spending and high taxes, which had been the norm since the Great Depression. By the mid-1970s, the conservative faction formerly headed by Robert Taft, and later by Barry Goldwater, found a new face to lead the party: Ronald Reagan.

Like the 1932 presidential election before, 1980 proved to be a redefining year in American politics, signifying the victory of the conservatives over the moderates and liberals within the Republican Party, as well as over the nation as a whole. Under Reagan, and later

George H.W. Bush and Speaker of the House Newt Gingrich, the Republicans moved to the right, promoting lower corporate taxes, an aggressive foreign policy with heavy military spending, a balanced budget, and welfare reform. Unlike their moderate predecessors, the Republicans of the 1980s and 90s disassociated with labor unions, promoting instead the growth of big business and Wall Street.

The party benefited dramatically during this period from support by the Religious Right, a movement made up of mostly Protestant Evangelicals who became heavily involved in politics and supported the conservative policies of the Republican Party. It was during this period that opposition to moral issues, such as abortion, drug use, contraception, homosexuality, and pornography, became strongly associated with the Republican Party.

By the end of the 20th century, the Republican Party had succeeded in balancing the federal budget for the first time in many decades by working with Democratic president Bill Clinton to reign in federal spending (particularly military and welfare spending). The late 1990s saw an economic boom that benefited both major parties and included a federal budget surplus. This set the stage for a hotly contested presidential election in 2000, together with an increasingly acrimonious political stalemate in Washington.

In that year, Republican George W. Bush, Texas governor and son of the first president Bush, ran for president against Clinton's vice-president, Democrat Al Gore. After a contentious campaign season, Gore managed to win the popular vote by more than 1.5 million votes, but lost the Electoral College vote after a recount in Florida was halted by the Supreme Court more than a month after the election. Problems with confusing ballots, particularly in Florida, led to widespread ballot reforms following the 2000 election.

Throughout the 21st century, the Republican Party has continued to be dominated by its conservative faction, with the ultra-conservative Tea Party Movement, which sprang up in 2009, being largely focused on reforming the policies of the party. Promoting small government, low taxes, a large military, and corporate growth, the party controlled much of Washington until the recession of 2008 swept the Democrats into power in both chambers of Congress and the presidency. Since then, the Republicans have fought an uphill battle against Democrat Barack Obama and a Democratic-led Congress, with opposition to a wide-sweeping Democratic reform of healthcare serving as the party's rallying cry (and the major impetus for the formation of the grassroots Tea Party Movement). Though candidate Mitt Romney lost the 2012 presidential election to Obama, the party finally gained control of both chamber of Congress in 2014.

By the Numbers:

The 20th and 21st Century Republican Party

Founded: circa 1854

Period of Activity: Ongoing

Party Slogans: "Get on a Raft With Taft" (1908); "America First" (1920); "Keep Cool With Coolidge" (1924); "I Like Ike" (1952); "Let's Make America Great Again" (1980); "Country First" (2008)

Number of Presidents: 12 (William McKinley, Theodore Roosevelt, William Howard Taft, Warren G. Harding, Calvin Coolidge, Herbert Hoover, Dwight D. Eisenhower, Richard Nixon, Gerald Ford, Ronald Reagan, George H.W. Bush, George W. Bush)

Leading Party Figures: Teddy Roosevelt, Herbert Hoover, Robert Taft (U.S. Senator from Ohio), Nelson Rockefeller (New York Governor and Vice-President under Gerald Ford), Richard Nixon, Ronald Reagan, Newt Gingrich (Speaker of the House during the 1990s), John Boehner (Speaker of the House during much of the Obama administration)

Main Platforms: Corporate interests, isolationism (early in the century), interventionism and large military, low taxes, small government, civil rights, balanced budgets, states' rights, welfare reform, moralism, national security/border control

THE 20ᵀᴴ and 21ˢᵗ CENTURY DEMOCRATIC PARTY

THE DEMOCRATIC Party spent the last half of the 19th century, and the first third of the 20th century as, essentially, the minority party in American politics. Split into geographic factions between Northern liberals and Southern conservatives, the party lacked the unity necessary to upend the power of the Republican Party, particularly in Washington.

In the early part of the 20th century, the Democrats were led by William Jennings Bryan, a noted speaker and perennial presidential candidate who campaigned on issues such as free silver, anti-imperialism, and trust-busting.

When the Republican Party split in 1912, former Princeton President and New Jersey governor Woodrow Wilson was elected to the White House. He went on to become the first Democrat elected to two consecutive terms since the original Democrat, Andrew Jackson, more than 80 years earlier. Also in 1912, congressional Democrats took advantage of the Republican split to take control of both chambers of Congress for the first time in almost twenty years.

Under Wilson, the Democrats were able to pass an unprecedented amount of legislation that the party had been pushing for many years. Among these were the creation of the Federal Reserve and Federal Trade Commission, stricter anti-trust laws, broad federal assistance to farmers, low tariffs to spur economic growth, and, notably, a federal income tax.

Prior to this time, the federal government had only imposed an income tax twice. The first time was during the Lincoln administration in the 1860s in an effort to raise money for the Union war effort. That tax eventually expired in the early 1870s. During the Cleveland administration of the mid-1890s, the first peace-time income tax was instituted, but it was declared unconstitutional by the Supreme Court in 1895.

This Supreme Court ruling set the stage for the proposal and eventual adoption of the 16th Amendment, which took place with bipartisan support in 1909 under William Howard Taft and a Republican Congress. This amendment effectively allowed the federal government to tax the income of individuals and corporations. While Democrats and other liberal groups had long spearheaded the movement for an income tax, there was wide support for it among Republicans of this era as well, thanks to the swell of progressive voices within the party.

It took four years for 36 states (three-fourths of the total, as required by the Constitution) to ratify the amendment, and it officially took effect in 1913, just a few days before Wilson was sworn into office.

Wilson and the Democratic-controlled Congress immediately went to work on legislation to enact a new income tax and adjust the tariff, and the result was the Revenue Act of 1913, which lowered tariffs to their lowest rates since before the Civil War, and established the first permanent income tax (with such a low tariff, an income tax was necessary to make up for the lost revenue).

The income tax began modestly: only single people making more than $3,000 per year (over $60,000 in today's dollars), and married couples making more than $4,000 per year, would be taxed, and the rate was just 1%. Starting at $20,000 (nearly half a million in today's economy), the rate rose to 2%, up through the $500,000 level (over $11 million today), where it topped out at 7%. (Today the lowest earners pay about 10% and the highest [over $400,000 per year] pay 39%.)

Prior to this time, the high tariff had always been the main source of money for the federal government. Starting with the Revenue Act of 1913, income tax would become the government's main way of funding itself.

In addition to this and other reforms, Wilson and the Democrats also passed bills enacting 8-hour workdays for railroad workers, as well as the Keating-Owen Act of 1916 which outlawed child labor. To Wilson's dismay, however, this law was ruled unconstitutional in 1918.

Republicans swept into power again in 1920, following Wilson's retirement, while the Democrats continued to struggle with geographic differences and suffer from a general distrust by the population at large. Northern Democrats were viewed as part of a corrupt political machine that dated back to the 19th century, while Southern Democrats were increasingly viewed as insular and too heavily influenced by the Ku Klux Klan, which reached its pinnacle in the 1920s.

Nowhere were the internal struggles of the Democrats more obvious than in the 1924 Democratic National Convention, where the two leading candidates represented the two dominant factions of the party: New York governor Al Smith, who was supported by urban liberals in the Northeast and Midwest, Catholics, ethnic minorities (including many Italian, German, and Irish Americans), and "wets;" while William Gibbs McAdoo of California (former Secretary of the Treasury and a son-in-law of Woodrow Wilson) had widespread support from "dry" white Protestants in the rural South, West, and Midwest.

The deep division among these two Democratic factions was illustrated when Smith's liberal delegates proposed a public condemnation of the Ku Klux Klan, something that outraged McAdoo's more conservative supporters. Fierce and bitter debate took place and the motion ultimately failed.

When it came time to actually vote on a nominee, more than 100 ballots were taken with neither candidate able to summon enough votes to win the nomination, making this convention, at fifteen days, the longest nominating convention in U.S. history. When it became apparent that many of the state delegations were running out of funds to remain at the convention, both candidates agreed to step aside, and, on the 103rd ballot, the Democrats compromised on John W. Davis of West Virginia. Davis, a former diplomat and congressman, was not widely known and lost in a landslide to incumbent Republican Calvin Coolidge.

It was ultimately the Great Depression that served to finally unite the Democrats and help sweep them into power in the realigning election of 1932. Not only did the Democrats place liberal Franklin D. Roosevelt into the White House, but they also won both chambers of Congress and a majority of the state gubernatorial elections. Under Roosevelt's "New Deal" economic policy, the government began taking a firmer role in economic regulation, backed by stronger social welfare programs.

Among the issues tackled by the New Deal was widespread banking and monetary reform, including the formation of the Federal Deposit Insurance Corporation, or FDIC, which helped to prevent the bank runs that had played such a significant and damaging role in the collapse of the economy a few years earlier. The New Deal also established the Social Security Administration, as well as plans to fight both rural and urban poverty, including the first Food Stamp program in U.S. history.

New Deal laws like the Wagner Act and the Fair Labor Standards Act (FLSA) strengthened the rights of labor unions and workers. Notably, the FLSA established a 44-hour workweek, a federal minimum wage (25 cents at the time), outlawed child labor, and established the notion of "time and a half" for any overtime worked.

Finally, the New Deal established the Works Progress Administration – a program that pumped billions of dollars into public works projects and infrastructure, providing millions of new jobs to the unemployed, and building countless roads, bridges, and schools throughout the United States.

The New Deal was such an ambitious and influential program that it essentially reshaped the entire political landscape. A "liberal" was now anyone who supported the New Deal and its ideologies; a "conservative," anyone who opposed it.

Coalitions ultimately formed around these two perspectives: the so-called New Deal Coalition included state Democratic organizations, labor unions and blue-collar workers, minorities (including religious minorities like Catholics and Jews), farmers and agricultural interests, intellectuals, urban dwellers, and some liberal Republicans; meanwhile, the Conservative Coalition that opposed the New Deal included most Republicans, as well as conservative Democrats (mostly in the South), Wall Street elites, business interests, and many white Protestants. This Conservative Coalition took control of Congress after 1938 and effectively put an end to any further New Deal legislation.

With the exception of Republican Dwight D. Eisenhower's two terms in the 1950s, the Democrats controlled the White House until the end of the 1960s. Furthermore, except for the 80th Congress from 1947-49, and the 83rd Congress from 1953-55, Democrats consistently controlled the House of Representatives from the early 1930s all the way up through the early 1990s. However, because most Southern Democrats voted more often with the Conservative Coalition, passage of liberal legislation was frequently contested and blocked through these years.

Thanks to a super-majority in both chambers of Congress in the mid-1960s (which resulted from the reinvigoration of the party brought by John F. Kennedy), Democrat Lyndon Johnson managed, for a brief time, to neutralize the power of the conservatives and pass a significant amount of domestic legislation which became known, collectively, as the Great Society. Patterned after Roosevelt's New Deal, this legislation included numerous civil rights and anti-poverty laws, overhauled the nation's educational program, enacted consumer protection laws, and established Medicare and Medicaid.

Following this brief period of strength, the Democratic Party began to splinter in the late 1960s, largely over the issue of civil rights and the Vietnam War. Once desegregation and civil rights became a central platform of the Democrats in the 1960s, many conservative Southern Democrats began to defect from the party, some joining the Republicans (and thereby swelling a small anti-civil rights faction within the Republican Party), while many joined third parties, most notably the pro-segregationist American Independent Party. The "Solid South," as it had once been known in Democratic circles, had begun to crumble.

By 1968, opposition to the Vietnam War had grown so strong, even among some Democrats, that Johnson opted not to run for re-election. Following the assassination later that year of Democratic candidate Robert Kennedy, Johnson's vice-president, Hubert Humphrey, won a hotly contested nominating convention. The general election proved very close between Humphrey and Republican Richard Nixon, with the two candidates separated by just 500,000 votes out of more than 73 million cast – less than 1% of the total. Nixon eked out small victories in California, Ohio, and Illinois, giving him enough electoral votes to win the election. Significantly, Humphrey lost every state in the traditionally Democratic South except for Texas, beginning a slow transformation of southern politics from liberal to conservative that would continue up through the end of the century and beyond.

Though Democrat Jimmy Carter won the presidency in 1976, thanks largely to the scandal-plagued Nixon administration and a vulnerable incumbent in Republican Gerald Ford, the Democrats spent most of the next 25 years controlling Congress – particularly the House of Representatives – under a succession of Republican presidents.

During the 1980s, in fact, so many Democrats voted for Republican Ronald Reagan that they were referred to as "Reagan Democrats." These Democrats, who were mostly white, working-class northerners, felt alienated from the Democratic Party because of its focus on minorities and the poor, and found the Republicans of the Reagan era to be more in line with their unique middle class concerns.

Though many of these defectors later returned to the Democratic Party, the Republicans had now gained a strong foothold among working class voters, a voting segment that had traditionally belonged almost exclusively to the Democrats.

As a result of the Reagan Revolution, the party made efforts to rebrand itself in the 1980s and 1990s, moving away from the left and more towards the center in an attempt to garner broader appeal. Though the strategy failed miserably in the election of 1988, with Reagan's vice-president, George Bush, easily defeating Democratic candidate Michael Dukakis, it paid off in 1992 when Bill Clinton, invigorating the party base, defeated Bush and third party candidate Ross Perot to take the White House.

The leader of the so-called "New Democrats," Clinton moved the party rightward on economic policy, working with a Republican Congress to balance the budget for the first time in more than 30 years, and championing the North American Free Trade Agreement (NAFTA) over the objections of labor unions. At the same time, the party remained true to many of its traditional platforms, including the rights of women and minorities (now including gay rights), healthcare reform, and stricter gun regulations.

Despite an impeachment trial, Clinton remained a popular president, leaving office at the end of the century with the highest approval rating of any president since Franklin Roosevelt. As we saw in the previous chapter, however, his popularity was not enough to ensure the victory of his vice-president in the 2000 election, though Al Gore, as we noted, did win the popular vote that year.

Following a 6-year period in which Republicans controlled both chambers of Congress and the White House, the Democrats finally won a majority in the House of Representatives in 2006, then gained the Senate as well in 2008, while Democrat Barack Obama won the presidency. The party, however, only controlled all three posts for one legislative term, as 2010 saw the Republicans retake control of the House of Representatives. During the first two years of Obama's presidency, however, the party did manage to pass a controversial, yet landmark, healthcare reform law that had been a top legislative desire for Democrats for several decades (a similar attempt to overhaul healthcare early in Bill Clinton's presidency was foiled by congressional Republicans).

Obama's presidency has been marred by low approval ratings and a partisan Congress that has managed to pass very little legislation since 2010, while the voting population, in general, has become heavily polarized and cynical. However, Obama won reelection in 2012 despite approval ratings that were below 50% for much of the campaign season.

By the Numbers:

The 20th and 21st Century Democratic Party

Founded: circa 1828

Period of Activity: Ongoing

Party Slogans: "Equal Rights to All, Special Privileges to None" (1900); "He [Wilson] Kept Us Out of War" (1916); "I Propose a New Deal" (1932); "LBJ for the USA" (1964); "It's the Economy, Stupid" (1992); "Yes We Can" (2008)

Number of Presidents: 8 (Woodrow Wilson, Franklin D. Roosevelt, Harry Truman, John F. Kennedy, Lyndon Johnson, Jimmy Carter, Bill Clinton, Barack Obama)

Leading Party Figures: William Jennings Bryan, Woodrow Wilson, Franklin D. Roosevelt, John William McCormack (Speaker of the House during the 1960s), Tip O'Neill (Speaker of the House during the Carter and Reagan years), Bill Clinton, Nancy Pelosi (Speaker of the House during the 2000s)

Main Platforms: Anti-trust laws, economic regulation, strong federal government, social welfare, civil rights, women's rights, interventionism/larger military, anti-poverty, labor unions, healthcare reform, gun control, marriage equality

THE STATES' RIGHTS DEMOCRATIC PARTY AND THE AMERICAN INDEPENDENT PARTY

THESE TWO parties were created by segregationist factions of the Democratic Party and used as a vehicle to support the presidential campaigns of two prominent segregationists: South Carolina's Strom Thurmond in 1948, and Alabama's George Wallace in 1968.

1948 was a watershed year in presidential politics, as Democrat Harry Truman attempted to legitimize his presidency by winning election to a full term (as vice-president, he had ascended to the Oval Office in 1945 following the death of Franklin Roosevelt). Like many vice-presidents-turned-president before him, Truman failed to win the support of many in his own party, leading to a 3-way split among the Democrats in 1948.

The liberal wing of the party split to form a short-lived reincarnation of the old Progressive Party, headed by Henry Wallace, a former vice-president under Franklin Roosevelt.

Meanwhile, the conservative wing of the party, made up exclusively of southern Democrats, split to form the States' Rights Democratic Party, led by South Carolina Governor Strom Thurmond.

The Dixiecrats, as the party was more commonly known, evolved out of a contentious Democratic National Convention in July of 1948. As the likely nominee, Truman introduced a moderate civil rights plank into the proposed Democratic platform. It was intended to placate both the conservative wing of the party, who wanted no civil rights plank at all, and the liberal wing of the party, who wanted radical civil rights proposals. Instead, neither side was happy, and in the end a more radical plank, authored by northern liberals, was adopted in a close vote.

Upon adoption of the plank, Strom Thurmond and several dozen of his southern supporters, walked out of the convention.

They immediately convened on their own and established the States' Rights Democratic Party, hoping to replace Truman with Governor Thurmond as the Democratic candidate on the ballots in the South. They ultimately succeeded in this effort in only four states – Louisiana, Mississippi, Alabama, and South Carolina. In those states, Thurmond was listed on the ballot as the Democratic candidate for president. Everywhere else, Thurmond was listed as a third party candidate for the Dixiecrats, or States' Rights Party.

The Dixiecrats were under no delusions that they could win the election outright. Like many third parties before them, they simply hoped to win enough electoral votes to force a run-off in what was sure to be a close election between Truman and the Republican nominee, Thomas Dewey. A run-off between the two men in the House of Representatives would force one or the other to offer concessions on civil rights issues to southern Democrats in exchange for their support in the run-off election. Regardless of who eventually won, it would put a hamper on civil rights legislation, and serve to show the Democratic Party that it could not operate effectively without its southern wing.

Following Thurmond's nomination, with Mississippi Governor Fielding Wright as his running mate, another convention was held in which an official party platform was adopted. In it, the Dixiecrats asserted that the platforms of both the Republican and Democratic parties called for a "police nation" ruled by a "totalitarian, centralized bureaucratic government." The platform went on to state:

We stand for the segregation of the races and the racial integrity of each race…We oppose the elimination of segregation [and] the repeal of miscegenation statutes [statutes outlawing biracial marriages]…We oppose and condemn the action of the Democratic Convention in sponsoring a civil rights program…[and] affirm that the effective enforcement of such a program would be utterly destructive of the social, economic and political life of the Southern people…

In the final tally on election night, Thurmond and the Dixiecrats managed to win all four states where they were listed as the main Democratic Party. It was the first time since 1892 that three different parties won at least four states in the general election. Despite their moderate success, they did not succeed in forcing a run-off election. Even though his party had split three ways, Truman surprised the media and all the pollsters by winning 303 electoral votes, well more than the 266 needed to win the election.

Following this, most of the Dixiecrats returned to the Democratic Party, but their short-lived protest represented the first cracks in the century-old Democratic hold over the southern states.

The American Independent Party was formed in 1967 in California as a far-right party supporting states' rights. They very quickly teamed up with George Wallace, a prominent segregationist and former governor of Alabama who had run for the Democratic nomination in 1964.

Though segregation and opposition to civil rights wasn't at the core of the party's founding, party leaders were perfectly happy to team up with the conservative Wallace, who they believed could provide prominence and legitimacy to their fledgling party.

After picking retired Air Force General Curtis LeMay as Wallace's running mate, the party immediately drafted and adopted a platform calling for, among other things, a permanent end to taxation, an end to poverty by means of the private sector (as opposed to public welfare), a firm stance on states' rights, and a "re-dedication…to the love of God and country" along with a judicial system that would remain "mindful of the attitudes of the people in this regard."

While not mentioning segregation explicitly, the platform accused the federal government under Democrat Lyndon Johnson of usurping the rights and privileges of the states. It condemned the "so-called" 1964 Civil Rights Act, which the platform asserted had "set race against race and class against class." The party promised to restore the "powers and authority" of state and local governments, so that they could control their own "internal affairs without interference…[from] the Federal Government." These passages were a thinly veiled attack on efforts by the Johnson administration to desegregate the South.

Wallace's goal was similar to that of Strom Thurmond twenty years earlier: win enough electoral votes in the South to throw the election to the House of Representatives, then use his influence to gain important concessions.

It almost worked.

Wallace managed to win more electoral votes than any third party candidate since Teddy Roosevelt in 1912, taking five states in the South and winning nearly 10 million votes overall. Republican Richard Nixon needed 270 electoral votes to win; he eked out victories over Wallace in North Carolina, South Carolina, and Tennessee by only a few percentage points each, putting him over the top.

Unlike the States' Rights Party before it, the American Independent Party continued on after Wallace's failed presidential bid. Throughout the 1970s and 1980s, the party consistently ran right-wing candidates in presidential elections, but also consistently got fewer and fewer votes in each election cycle. In 1992, the party was absorbed by the burgeoning Constitution Party, officially becoming the Constitution Party's California chapter. In 2008, the party split, and its national status is still in dispute as of this writing.

By the Numbers:

The States' Rights Democratic Party

Founded: 1948

Period of Activity: 1948 presidential election

Party Slogans: "Get In the Fight For States' Rights"

Number of Presidents: 0 (Strom Thurmond was the party's only presidential nominee)

Leading Party Figures: Strom Thurmond, Fielding Wright, Leander Perez (Louisiana political boss and district judge), Harry Byrd (U.S. Senator from Virginia), Ross Lillard (party president)

Main Platforms: Segregation, opposition to civil rights legislation, states' rights

By the Numbers:

The American Independent Party

Founded: 1967

Period of Activity: About twenty-five years on the national level (absorbed into the Constitution Party in 1992)

Party Slogans: "Stand Up For America"

Number of Presidents: 0 (George Wallace in 1968 and John Schmitz in 1972 were the party's only candidates who earned more than one million votes in a presidential election)

Leading Party Figures: George Wallace, Bill Shearer (party founder), Lester Maddox (governor of Georgia, segregationist, and the party's 1976 presidential nominee), Ed Noonan (party chairman and perennial candidate for California state offices in the 2000s)

Main Platforms: Ultra conservative policies, states' rights, tax reform, religious freedom, pro-gun, pro-life, anti-gay marriage

THE LIBERTARIAN PARTY

THE LIBERTARIAN Party was founded in Colorado in 1971 as a reaction to what its founders perceived to be an increasing loss of American liberties, spurred by opposition to the Vietnam War and, especially, the elimination of the gold standard.

As we saw in a previous chapter, the gold standard had been in place in American economics since the 19th century and, after a protracted political fight, became official policy at the beginning of the 20th. By the late 1960s and early 1970s, however, problems were beginning to develop.

Following World War Two, a new international monetary system, based on the U.S. gold standard, was enacted among the major industrialized nations of the world. Known as the Bretton Woods System (because the terms of the agreement had been hammered out at Bretton Woods, New Hampshire, in 1944), the system sought to stabilize foreign exchange rates by allowing foreign markets to convert the U.S. dollar directly to gold. In short, foreign currencies were valued against the dollar, and the dollar was backed by gold. The intention was to avoid the massive economic depressions that had occurred across Europe following World War One, and which had created the conditions that led to World War Two.

The system worked well in its early years, helping to rebuild Europe and Japan and leading to an economic boom in the United States as foreign markets were flooded with American-made products.

However, by the 1960s, Europe and the Far East had long since recovered from the devastation of World War Two, and America was no longer the only major economic power on the international stage. The country's share of the world's economy had dropped significantly, and together with other factors such as the high cost of the Vietnam War and inflation, the U.S. dollar was quickly losing its value and becoming unstable. Furthermore, because of the growth of the world economy, U.S. gold reserves could now only back a fraction of foreign holdings.

When some European countries, sensing an economic crisis, began to demand gold in exchange for their U.S. dollars in the summer of 1971, U.S. president Richard Nixon acted decisively. In August, he issued an executive order that suspended the right of foreign markets to exchange U.S. dollars for gold. Though the move was intended at first to be temporary, providing time for a new international agreement, the whole Bretton Woods system had collapsed by 1973. In time, every major country, including the U.S., left the gold standard and allowed their currencies to become free-floating – that is, no longer fixed to the value of another currency, and backed only by the faith and credit of the government that issues it.

The elimination of the gold standard proved to be a major impetus for the creation of the Libertarian Party. Its founders especially took issue with the price controls enacted by Nixon as part of his August 1971 executive order. For 90 days following the elimination of the gold standard, wages, salaries, and prices for commodities were frozen, to prevent sudden inflation. A year earlier, Congress had given Nixon the right to take such action, and the founders of the Libertarian Party believed such powers demonstrated a federal government that had become too centralized and too powerful. It was, for them, the last straw.

As its name implies, the Libertarian Party was founded on the principle of personal liberties and freedoms. Throughout the last part of the 20th century, the party quickly rose to become the largest third party in the United States, frequently drawing members from both the political left and right. Socially liberal and fiscally conservative, the party supported traditional liberal causes such as the legalization of marijuana, marriage rights for all people, and abortion rights, while also campaigning for traditional conservative policies like limited regulation of the free market, low taxes, and the elimination of welfare. The party also took a strong anti-war stance and pushed for a non-interventionist foreign policy.

Though the party was still in its infancy in 1972, it nominated a California philosophy professor named John Hospers for the presidency. His running mate was a businesswoman and journalist named Tonie Nathan. The party only managed to get their ticket on the ballot in two states, and received just a few thousand votes. However, an elector in Virginia, pledged to Richard Nixon, cast his Electoral College vote for the Hospers ticket, giving the Libertarians their first (and to date, only) electoral vote. More significantly, it marked the first time in U.S. history that a female candidate on a presidential ticket received an electoral vote.

Since that time, the party has run candidates in every presidential election, as well as all other levels of federal, state, and local government. Though no Libertarian has ever won a seat in the U.S. House or Senate, several have served in state legislatures, and hundreds have been elected or appointed to positions within state and local governments.

During the 1980 presidential election, the party gained ballot access in all 50 states, the first third party to do so since the Socialist Party in 1916. Their candidate, California lawyer Ed Clark, won almost a million votes and more than 1% of the popular vote – the party's best showing to date (candidate Gary Johnson won more popular votes in the 2012 presidential election, but less of the overall percentage).

The 1990s saw continued growth and mainstream recognition for the party, with Libertarian candidates collectively earning millions of votes in each major election year, and hundreds of candidates winning offices in state and local elections. Party activists helped to block the Clinton administration's attempt to reform the nation's healthcare, believing it constituted a government takeover of the healthcare system, and successfully lobbied against proposed banking regulations they believed would have compromised privacy rights.

As the century came to an end, the Libertarian Party had established itself as the largest, most prominent, and most influential third party in American politics, a position it still owns to the present day. According to the party's website, there are currently 152 Libertarians holding offices among 33 states.

By the Numbers:

The Libertarian Party

Founded: 1971

Period of Activity: Ongoing

Party Slogans: "Individual Liberty, Personal Responsibility;" "Free Will, Free Markets, Personal Responsibility;" "Live Free"

Number of Presidents: 0 (Gary Johnson, in 2012, earned 1.2 million popular votes, the most for any Libertarian presidential candidate to date)

Leading Party Figures: David Nolan (party founder and national chairman), Ed Crane (political activist, party chairman, and founder of a Libertarian think-tank called the Cato Institute), John Hospers, David Koch (billionaire businessman, political activist, and 1980 Libertarian vice-presidential candidate), Ron Paul (Republican congressman who ran for president as a Libertarian in 1988), Harry Browne (presidential candidate in 1996 and 2000).

Main Platforms: Personal, corporate, and civil liberties, small government, small military, neutrality in foreign affairs, abortion rights, legalization of recreational drugs, free trade, open immigration, abolition of marriage as a legal contract, support of same-sex unions, elimination of income tax

THE REFORM PARTY

THE REFORM Party was founded in 1995 as a vehicle for the presidential campaign of Texas billionaire Ross Perot. As an Independent in the 1992 presidential election, Perot had garnered 20 million votes, nearly 20% of the total cast that year, giving him the most votes ever for a third party candidate, and the largest percentage of the popular vote for such a candidate since Teddy Roosevelt's third party run in 1912.

Perot came to prominence in 1992 with promises of high ethical standards and fiscal reforms. Promising to balance the federal budget, reform tax codes, push for congressional term limits, and reform campaign finance laws, Perot proved a popular candidate among voters looking for a change in the status quo.

Following the 1992 election, many of the issues Perot campaigned on were taken up by Congress. However, proposed constitutional amendments to require a balanced budget and to limit congressional terms to 12 years (two terms for a senator, six terms for a representative) failed to gain enough votes. As a result, Perot supporters, particularly those affiliated with his lobbying group known as United We Stand America, began organizing a new party to continue pushing for these and other reforms. The name they chose for the party reflected the group's basic ideology of reforming what they saw as a broken system in Washington.

Perot was the obvious choice for the new party's first presidential ticket in 1996, though he initially declined to run. After he finally entered the race, he easily won the nomination; however, supporters of another candidate – former Colorado governor Richard Lamm – accused the Perot faction of rigging the votes and walked out of the party's national convention. They eventually formed a splinter group called the American Reform Party.

Due to new rules governing debate procedures, Perot was not able to take part in the presidential debates in 1996, as he had done to such wide acclaim in 1992. He still managed to win more than 8 million votes in the general election, but finished a distant third to Bill Clinton and Bob Dole.

Following the 1996 election, the party struggled to maintain itself as some supporters left to join the American Reform Party faction, believing that the Reform Party itself was little more than Perot's own political machine. When former pro wrestler Jesse Ventura, however, won the gubernatorial race in Minnesota as a Reform Party candidate in 1998, new life was breathed into the party. Unfortunately, tensions between Ventura's supporters and the Perot faction eventually led Ventura to resign his membership just two years later.

In that same year, 2000, the party was further weakened when another split occurred over the party's presidential nomination. Perot had earned enough votes as the Reform Party candidate in 1996 to qualify the party for federal campaign funds for the 2000 presidential election. The conservative faction of the party supported former Republican presidential candidate Pat Buchanan for the presidency, while the moderates and liberals preferred physicist John Hagelin. After a bitter primary season, the two factions split during the national convention and each nominated their own man. Since more than $12 million was a stake in federal campaign funds, the courts had to work the issue out, eventually ruling in favor of Buchanan.

Though he earned less than one-half of one percent of the popular vote, his peculiarly high vote total in Palm Beach County, Florida, may have changed the outcome of the close election between George W. Bush and Al Gore. Florida ultimately determined the winner of that year's election, and the final vote difference between the two major candidates in Florida was less than 600 votes. Though he earned only 0.3% of the vote statewide, Buchanan earned more than twice that much in Palm Beach County, enough to have changed the outcome of the entire election. Both Buchanan and representatives from Florida's chapter of the Reform Party have asserted that a confusing ballot (the so-called "Butterfly Ballot") almost certainly led Buchanan to earn several thousand extra votes in Palm Beach County that were likely intended for Gore. Had Gore gotten those votes, he would have won Florida and the presidency.

Following Buchanan's presidential campaign, the conservative faction took control of the party for the next two years, until Buchanan left to rejoin the Republican Party. After that, the party moved back towards the left, becoming more centrist in it platforms and philosophies, continuing to push for campaign finance reform, a balanced budget amendment, and congressional term limits. The party has continued nominating candidates in presidential elections throughout the 2000s, though they have not made any national headlines. Political activist Ralph Nader won almost half a million votes in 2004, but in both 2008 and 2012, the party's candidates earned less than 1000 votes each.

By the Numbers:

The Reform Party

Founded: 1995

Period of Activity: Ongoing

Party Slogans: "Honest Leadership, Real Solutions"

Number of Presidents: 0 (Ross Perot's 1996 presidential run was by far the best showing in the party's history)

Leading Party Figures: Ross Perot, Jesse Ventura, Pat Buchanan, Pat Choate (vice-presidential nominee in 1996 with Perot, and party chairman in the 2000s) Ted Weill (2008 presidential nominee and state party chairman in Mississippi)

Main Platforms: Campaign finance reform including the elimination of Political Action Committees, constitutional amendments requiring a balanced budget and limiting congressional terms, opposition to free trade agreements in order to protect U.S. jobs, direct election of the president by popular vote, tax reform, secure borders

THE CONSTITUTION PARTY

THE 1990s saw the organization and formation of two third parties that have grown in prominence throughout the first decade and a half of the 21st century: the Constitution Party and the Green Party. Together with the Libertarian Party and the Reform Party, they represent the most prominent alternatives to the mainstream Democratic and Republican parties.

The Constitution Party was founded in 1991 as the U.S. Taxpayer's Party. The party's founder, Howard Phillips, once worked in the Nixon administration, but resigned in protest when Nixon failed to veto continued funding for various government programs enacted under Democrat Lyndon Johnson.

Described by the Southern Poverty Law Center (a civil rights organization that tracks hate groups) as "far-right" and "extremist," the Constitution Party has more than 350,000 registered members, making it the third largest political party, by registered affiliation, in the United States.

The party's platform asserts that, since the United States was founded "by Christians…on a foundation of Christian principles," and since the Constitution "established a Republic rooted in Biblical law," the goal of the party is to "restore American jurisprudence to its Biblical foundations." As the present party name (adopted in 1999) implies, it pushes for a strict reading of the Constitution, aiming to dramatically limit the powers of the federal government. It considers itself the "philosophical home" of the Tea Party Movement – the grassroots political movement that sprang up in the wake of the 2008 economic crisis and the election of Democrat Barack Obama to the presidency.

Its current platform refers to illegal immigration as an "invasion," and calls on the U.S. military to secure state and national borders. It rejects calls for amnesty to illegal aliens, and disapproves of the practice of offering citizenship to children born in the United States to illegal parents. It also calls for a moratorium on *all* immigration (including legal immigration), except in "extreme hardship cases," until federal subsidies to immigrants have been ended and "proper security procedures" have been put into place to protect against "terrorist infiltration." The party also calls for English to be made the nation's official language, arguing that the ability to speak English should be a prerequisite for citizenship.

The platform opposes same-sex marriage, all abortion for any reason, and favors the outlawing of pornography, arguing that First Amendment rights do not extend to obscenity. Without actually arguing against federal anti-drug laws, the party's platform urges states, rather than the federal government, to "restrict access to drugs and enforce such restrictions."

The party's platform calls for unrestricted gun rights for "law-abiding citizens," demanding a complete repeal of "all federal firearms legislation."

The party opposes foreign intervention and trade agreements, favoring instead a tariff system to protect American industry and raise funds for the government. The party's platform calls for an end to the federal income tax.

The party supports a large military, but only for national defense, arguing that the U.S. has no business involving itself in foreign wars. It argues against women in the military, stating that "the radical feminization of the military...undermine(s) the integrity, morale, and performance of our military." It also argues for the establishment of regulated state militias, as well as the arming of private citizens for local protection ("unorganized militia at the county and community level").

The Constitution Party opposes federal welfare programs for individuals, arguing that federal welfare is unconstitutional, specifically stating that government redistribution of wealth is a form of theft, which it notes is condemned by Biblical teachings. Instead, the platform calls upon Christian values to undergird private charitable giving as a means of replacing welfare.

Finally, the party supports and has called for the impeachment of Barack Obama, citing the issuing of executive orders, sending troops into foreign combat zones without a declaration of war by Congress, and collaborating with the United Nations. It believes each of these actions is unconstitutional and represents an abuse of power by the Executive Branch.

Founder Howard Phillips was the party's presidential candidate in 1992, 1996, and 2000, with his best showing coming in 1996, when he received some 182,000 votes nationwide. Chuck Baldwin, a Florida evangelical pastor and former chairman of Florida's chapter of the fundamentalist Christian organization Moral Majority, earned nearly 200,000 votes as the party's candidate in 2008. 2012 proved a down year for the party: the presidential ticket, led by former Democratic congressman Virgil Goode, only made it onto the ballot in 26 states, the lowest ballot distribution for the party since its inception in 1992.

By the Numbers:

The Constitution Party

Founded: 1991

Period of Activity: Ongoing

Party Slogans: "Fighting for America's Future;" "The Real Conservatives"

Number of Presidents: 0 (based on percentages, the party's best showing was in 1996, when Howard Phillips earned 0.19% of the total popular vote)

Leading Party Figures: Howard Phillips, Chuck Baldwin, Frank Fluckiger (national party chairman), Virgil Goode, Peter Gemma (member of the party's Executive Committee and a known white-supremacist)

Main Platforms: Right-wing policies, nationalism, isolationism, anti-tax, anti-federal government, pro-gun, anti-immigration, strict constitutionalism, Christian moralism

THE GREEN PARTY

THE GREEN Party was founded in 1991 in order to unite various "Green" organizations from around the country. The Green Movement had begun in the 1980s as a way of bringing together socially liberal, environmental, and pacifist ideologies. By 1990, a split had occurred among members over whether the movement should pursue elected office, or work instead at the grassroots level to lobby for change. The Greens/Green Party USA was founded in 1991 in an attempt to reconcile the two sides. In 1996, however, various independent, state-level Green parties came together to form the Association of State Green Parties, which later changed its name to the Green Party of the United States. The two organizations have operated side-by-side since then, though the Greens/Green Party USA is no longer registered as a political party, but instead operates solely as a political advocacy group.

The current Green Party platform calls for a number of liberal and libertarian reforms within the government, the economy, the environment, and society. It outlines "ten key values" that include grassroots democracy, social justice, ecological wisdom, nonviolence, diversity, and the decentralization of both the government and the economy.

Among other things, the Green Party advocates the abolition of the Electoral College, in favor of the direct election of the president by popular vote; public (rather than corporate and private) funding for all elections, including equal airtime on radio and television for all qualified candidates; reclamation of the airwaves by the public, using anti-trust laws to "carve up big media conglomerates," which the platform argues are "too cozy with the economic and political elites;" and the prohibition of commercial advertising to children under the age of 12 years.

The Green Party believes the U.S. should abide more rigidly to the guidelines of the United Nations, deferring to the U.N. to settle foreign disputes and to lead the charge on foreign military intervention. The party calls for a "no-first-strike" and "no-preemptive-strike" policy for the U.S. military, as well as an end to the stockpiling of chemical and biological weapons. The platform also calls for the reduction of the U.S. defense budget by half, as well as diverting much of those funds to help support the needy.

The party advocates for a "fair distribution of income," arguing that the rich cannot be counted on to "regulate their profit-making excesses for the good of society." Without actually stating what constitutes "excessive," the platform proposes taxing the super-wealthy more heavily in order to "restrict the accumulation of excessive individual wealth."

Finally, the Green Party advocates providing free tuition to all students at public universities and colleges, as well as forgiving existing student loans. The party also advocates for private health insurance to be replaced by a universal, single-payer system funded through the federal government.

In 1996, still using the Association of State Green Parties name, the Greens nominated political activist Ralph Nader for president. He was nominated again in 2000, where he earned more than 2 million votes and was accused by supporters of Democrat Al Gore of spoiling Gore's near-victory (the assumption being that, had Nader dropped out of the race, his voters would have cast ballots for Gore instead, easily giving him the victory).

Green Party voting totals dropped in the 2004 and 2008 elections, but rebounded to nearly half a million in 2012 when Massachusetts physician Jill Stein was the party's nominee.

By the Numbers:

The Green Party

Founded: 1991

Period of Activity: Ongoing

Party Slogans: "A Green New Deal For America"

Number of Presidents: 0 (the party's best showing was in 2000, when it earned nearly 3% of the popular vote).

Leading Party Figures: Ralph Nader, Pat LaMarche (co-chairwoman on the party's National Committee, and vice-presidential candidate in 2004), Winona LaDuke (two-time vice-presidential candidate), Farheen Hakeem (political activist and party leader)

Main Platforms: Left-wing policies, universal healthcare, environmentalism, small military, social justice, women's rights, civil rights, marriage equality, nonviolence

AFTERWORD

As I hope this brief survey of American political parties has shown, there are two kinds of political parties in the United States: minor parties who come onto the scene with a specific ideology and agenda, and typically fade out after time, and our two major political parties, whose ideologies and agendas are constantly changing and evolving so that, from era to era, it can sometimes be hard to tell them apart.

Both the Republican Party and the Democratic Party have gone through periods of liberalism and conservatism, and both parties have always had liberal, moderate, and conservative factions. For instance, of the 11 Republicans who served as president during the 20th century, at least four were moderate-to-liberal, and by today's standards would fit well within the moderate wing of the Democratic Party (Teddy Roosevelt, Eisenhower, Nixon, and Ford). Similarly, a Democrat like Grover Cleveland, who supported fiscal conservatism and frequently used his veto powers to limit the reach of the federal government, looks far more like a Republican by today's standards than a Democrat. So do the southern Democrats of the mid-20th century, who pushed for states' rights and a limited federal government and were thus some of the most conservative members of Congress in that otherwise liberal era.

The two major parties have also, over the decades, switched positions on a variety of topics. Throughout much of the 20th century, the Republican Party was the party that pushed for a small military and an isolationist approach to foreign matters. Democrats, on the other hand, led us into all four of the 20th century's major wars – Wilson in World War One, Franklin Roosevelt in World War Two, Truman in Korea, and Johnson in Vietnam. Republicans, on the other hand, were elected to lead us *out* of two of those wars (Korea and Vietnam). Today, of course, both parties generally support foreign military intervention, but it is the Democratic Party today who pushes for a smaller military, while the Republican Party supports a much larger military budget and has led us into each of the last three major military conflicts – the Gulf War and the wars in Iraq and Afghanistan.

Additionally, throughout much of the 19th century (as well as among those aforementioned southern Democrats in the mid-20th century), the Democratic Party was generally seen as the party of rural America, supporting rural concerns over urban ones, and most widely supported in agricultural areas. Republicans, on the other hand, were, for many decades in the 19th and 20th centuries, the party of urban elites. Today, those roles have switched, with Republicans enjoying their widest support in rural areas, and Democrats holding majority support in cities and large metropolitan areas. Similarly, the Democratic Party used to be the home of many evangelical Protestants like Southern Baptists and Pentecostals, while the Republican Party had broader support among mainline Protestants like Methodists and Presbyterians. Today, those roles have largely switched, with mainline Protestants more apt to vote Democratic, and evangelical Protestants giving wide support to Republicans.

Regardless of how our two main parties have switched roles over the decades, both parties today have at least one thing in common: rampant partisanship. It would be short-sighted, of course, to assume that partisanship is a modern phenomenon, and I hope the preceding look at America's political party history has proven that. Be that as it may, it seems clear that partisanship has been on the rise in U.S. politics for at least two decades now, with both major parties digging in their heels and standing firm on their ideologies. In the last few years in particular, the rise of the Tea Party has helped foster this spirit of partisanship as it has pushed the Republican Party rightward, though the Tea Party is undoubtedly a result, and not a cause, of partisanship in American politics.

So what are the causes of this rise in partisanship? A lot of it has to do with money and the growing power of each party's ideological base. Members of Congress are tied closely to financially-powerful special interest groups who help fund their campaigns, and this, together with fear of alienating their heavily partisan base, moves them away from the center and towards the fringes of the political spectrum.

Another facet of partisanship, among voters themselves, comes from the flow and availability of information in the modern world, where we are all inundated with different opinions in a constant stream, and everyone can find a partisan niche to wall up around themselves. There has never been a time in U.S. history when so much information and so many different perspectives were so available on such a large scale. Anyone looking for like-minded individuals can find them in the instantaneous click of a mouse, smart phone, radio dial, or remote control button.

Finally, our population growth undoubtedly has played a role in the rise of partisanship. The U.S. population is currently around 320 million people. That's nearly 100 million more than in 1980. We've grown by nearly 35 million people just since the year 2000. The U.S., in fact, has the third largest population on earth. With that many people, living in a society where information flows at the speed of light, even fringe ideologies can find traction and support. Even if just one-half of one percent of Americans supports a given political ideology, that still creates a group more than a *million* people strong. And a million people can certainly influence the political discussion.

The simple fact is, we seem to be outgrowing the two-party system that has served us so well for so many decades. As noted, the U.S. is the third largest country on earth by population, yet we are one of the few democracies in the world functioning within a two-party system. Indeed, a brief Google search on this topic indicates that the only other countries on earth dominated by a two-party system are Jamaica and Malta – two tiny island nations. The democratic countries of Europe, Africa, Asia, and South America all have multi-party systems, where three or more political parties play a role in governing, routinely winning seats in the national government. And this is despite the fact that all but one of these countries has a significantly smaller population than the United States (India is much larger than the United States, but it also has dozens of national and state-based political parties).

Consider our northern neighbors in Canada. Canada has roughly 35 million people – just a fraction of the U.S. population (recall that the U.S. has added 35 million people in just the last fifteen years). Despite this, Canada currently has five political parties represented in their national parliament, as well as a handful of Independents.

In the U.S., our third parties can certainly influence discussions and policy-making, but they do not win national elections, nor are they represented in Congress. They simply can't compete with the enormous money, power, and brand of the Republican and Democratic parties.

Perhaps more than anything else, it is this entrenched two-party system that has paralyzed so much of our politics in recent years. Our federal government has become increasingly ineffective largely because the only two parties represented in Washington have become so bloated with money, power, and ties to special interests. Two parties simply cannot represent the diverse views of 320 million Americans. The United States Congress, I am convinced, would be much more effective with a slate of various political parties representing Americans from left to right across the political spectrum. Instead, we have just two parties, entrenched on the left and right, facing off like two early 20th century armies, with the American public caught in No Man's Land between.

With this in mind, how can we achieve a multi-party system? If voters would simply choose third party candidates instead of major party candidates, things might begin to change. However, expecting voters to spontaneously start voting third party is unrealistic, particularly with the advertising and brand power of the Republicans and Democrats. No, the only way this situation will change is through election reform and changes in the way campaigns are financed. We must pass laws that will even the playing field for all viable political parties. We must ensure that all recognized parties are equally funded, without the untold millions flowing in from special interests. And we must give equal advertising time on radio and television to all candidates.

Until and unless we make these changes, there is little hope for a break in the political stalemate that has become our new normal in American politics.

Did you enjoy this book on the history of American political parties? If so, show your support for this independent author by telling your friends about it and leaving a review at Amazon.com!

BIBLIOGRAPHY

Anbinder, Tyler. *Nativism and Slavery: The Northern Know Nothings and the Politics of the 1850s*

Andersen, Kristi. *The Creation of a Democratic Majority, 1928–1936*

Baker, Jean. *Affairs of Party: The Political Culture of Northern Democrats in the Mid-Nineteenth Century*

Bowen, Michael. *The Roots of Modern Conservatism: Dewey, Taft, and the Battle for the Soul of the Republican Party*

Chambers, William Nisbet, and Burnham, Walter Dean, eds. *The American Party Systems: Stages of Political Development*

Critchlow, Donald T. *The Conservative Ascendancy: How the Republican Right Rose to Power in Modern America*

Dawson, Matthew Q. *Partisanship and the Birth of America's Second Party, 1796-1800: Stop the Wheels of Government*

Earle, Jonathan Halperin. *Jacksonian Antislavery and the Politics of Free Soil, 1824–1854*

Edwards, Rebecca. *Angels in the Machinery: Gender in American Party Politics from the Civil War to the Progressive Era*

Eichengreen, Barry, and Flandreau, Marc. *The Gold Standard in Theory and History*

Elkins, Stanley M., and McKitrick, Eric. *The Age of Federalism*

Eyal, Yonatan. *The Young America Movement and the Transformation of the Democratic Party, 1828–1861*

Fischer, David Hackett. *The Revolution of American Conservatism: The Federalist Party in the Era of Jeffersonian Democracy*

Foner, Eric. *Free Soil, Free Labor, Free Men: The Ideology of the Republican Party before the Civil War*

Gienapp, William E. *Origins of the Republican Party, 1852–1856*

Gould, Lewis L. *America in the Progressive Era, 1890 – 1914*

Ibid. *Four Hats in the Ring: The 1912 Election and the Birth of Modern American Politics*

Hammond, Bray. *Banks and Politics in America from the Revolution to the Civil War*

Haynes, Stan M. *The First American Political Conventions: Transforming Presidential Nominations, 1832-1872*

Hofstadter, Richard. *The Idea of a Party System: The Rise of Legitimate Opposition in the United States, 1780–1840*

Holt, Michael F. *The Rise and Fall of the American Whig Party: Jacksonian Politics and the Onset of the Civil War*

Howe, Daniel Walker. *What Hath God Wrought: The Transformation of America, 1815-1848*

Kleppner, Paul. *The Third Electoral System 1853–1892: Parties, Voters, and Political Cultures*

Leuchtenburg, William E. *In the Shadow of FDR: From Harry Truman to George W. Bush*

Martis, Kenneth C. *The Historical Atlas of Political Parties in the United States Congress: 1789-1989*

McCarthy, Charles. *The Antimasonic Party: A Study of Political Antimasonry in the United States, 1827–1840*

Milkis, Sidney M. *The President and the Parties: The Transformation of the American Party System Since the New Deal*

Parsons, Lynn H. *The Birth of Modern Politics: Andrew Jackson, John Quincy Adams, and the Election of 1828*

Potter, David. *The Impending Crisis 1848–1861*

Rhodes, James Ford. *The History of the United States from the Compromise of 1850*

Rutland, Robert Allen. *The Democrats: From Jefferson to Clinton*

Schlesinger, Jr., Arthur Meier, ed. *History of American Presidential Elections, 1789–2000*

Ibid. *History of U.S. Political Parties*

Summers, Mark Wahlgren. *Rum, Romanism & Rebellion: The Making of a President, 1884*

Sundquist, James L. *Dynamics of the Party System: Alignment and Realignment of Political Parties in the United States*

Wilentz, Sean. *The Age of Reagan: A History 1974-2008*

Ibid. *The Rise of American Democracy: Jefferson to Lincoln*

Witcover, Jules. *Party of the People: A History of the Democrats*

ABOUT THE AUTHOR

B. Scott Christmas is a writer and historian originally from Lexington, Kentucky. The author of five novels and more than 500 poems, he has a degree in European History from Georgetown College, where he also studied Music and Creative Writing. An avid reader and blogger who speaks three languages, his research interests include Christian Origins and historical Jesus scholarship, as well as American Politics, Ancient Egypt, Medieval Europe, and the British Monarchy. He also writes music and plays three instruments. He lives with his wife and children in Cincinnati, Ohio.

Readers can visit his blog, Serene Musings, at www.serene-musings.blogspot.com.

BOOKS BY B. SCOTT CHRISTMAS

Christianity is a Verb
The Virgin Birth: Miracle or Legend?
The Life, Death, and Modern Discovery of Tutankhamun: A Brief Historical Narrative
Tragedy in the Sierra Nevada: A Narrative of the Donner Party
Washington's Nightmare: A Brief History of American Political Parties
Serendipity...And Other Stories
Widow's Walk (short story)
Serendipity (short story)
Walkabout: A Thriller

To find these titles, visit the B. Scott Christmas author page at Amazon.com.

Made in the USA
Monee, IL
11 October 2020